The Cross before Constantine

The Cross before Constantine

The Early Life of a Christian Symbol

Bruce W. Longenecker

Fortress Press
Minneapolis

THE CROSS BEFORE CONSTANTINE

The Early Life of a Christian Symbol

Cover design: Laurie Ingram

Cover image: Charcoal cross © Bruce Longenecker

Library of Congress Cataloging-in-Publication Data is available

Print ISBN: 978-1-4514-9030-5

eISBN: 978-1-5064-0036-5

The paper used in this publication meets the minimum requirements of American National Standard for Information Sciences — Permanence of Paper for Printed Library Materials, ANSI Z329.48-1984.

Manufactured in the U.S.A.

This book was produced using PressBooks.com, and PDF rendering was done by PrinceXML.

For Richard and Delia,
whose love and support has shown no bounds
throughout the years.

Contents

Preliminaries

Several colleagues at Baylor University and beyond have been helpful in the crafting of this project at one point or another—in particular, Michelle Brown, Everett Ferguson, Simon Gathercole, David Jeffrey, David Moessner, Mike Parsons, Jeffrey Spier, Todd Still, David Wilhite, and Tom Wright. Several Ph.D. students at Baylor University offered feedback on versions of the project: Jeremiah Bailey, David Beary, Scott Ryan, and Mike Whitenton.

This study was supported by the funders of the W. W. Melton Chair of Religion at Baylor University, by the Department of Religion at Baylor University, and by funds from the University Research Committee and the Vice Provost for Research at Baylor University.

Princeton University Press granted permission to reproduce the images in figures 3.1 through 3.5 and figures 5.6 and 5.7 (scanned from Jack Finegan, *The Archaeology of the New Testament: The Life of Jesus and the Beginning of the Early Church* [Princeton, NJ: Princeton University Press, 1992]). Permission to use figures 1.8 and 5.2 was granted by the Superintendency of Archaeological Heritage of Rome and Ostia Antica. Jeffrey Spier kindly granted permission to use the images in figures 5.8, 5.10, and 6.7, and supplied the original digital photos of those artifacts. The Museum of Fine Arts Boston granted permission to reproduce the image in figure 5.9. The British Museum granted permission to reproduce the image in figure 5.16 (British Museum MME 1986.05.01.1; courtesy of the Trustees of the British Museum). The Israel Exploration Society granted permission to reproduce the image in figure 5.17 (from Joseph Zias and Eliezer Sekeles, "The Crucified Man from Giv'at ha-Mivtar: A Reappraisal," *Israel Exploration Journal* 35 [1985]: 22–27). Cambridge University Press granted permission to reproduce the images in figures 5.20 and 5.21 (scanned from William M. Calder, "Early-Christian Epitaphs from Phrygia," *Anatolian Studies* 5 [1955]: 25–38). Barbara McManus provided the photo for figure 6.5, on behalf of the VRoma Project (www.vroma.org). The Ministry of Cultural Heritage, Activities and Tourism—Special Superintendency for Archaeological Heritage of Pompeii, Herculaneum and Stabiae granted permission to reproduce the images in figures 6.1, 6.3, 6.5 (compare 6.6), 6.8, 8.2, and 8.3. The reproduction or duplication of these images is prohibited.

Images (except for those listed above and those credited in footnotes) were photographed or produced as follows: Bruce Longenecker: figures 1.1 through 1.9; 3.1; 5.1, 2, 4, 5, 18, 19; 6.2, 8, 9; 8.1, 2, 3; Callum Longenecker: 6.1; Torrin Longenecker: 6.3; Fiona Bond: 6.4. Objects reproduced in the following images are from the author's private collection: figures 1.1 through 1.7, and 8.1.

The author and publisher gratefully acknowledge the permissions granted to reproduce the copyright material in this book. Every effort has been made to trace copyright holders and to obtain their permission for the use of copyright material. The author and publisher would welcome notification of any corrections that should be incorporated in future reprints or editions of this book.

Ancient literary works are referred to by established English titles, except in instances where English titles are not standard—in accord with the practice established by *The SBL Handbook of Style*, ed.

Patrick H. Alexander et al. (Peabody, MA: Hendrickson, 1999). In those instances, the Latin titles are used. Abbreviations are generally absent from this book, except in the following two instances.

CIL   *Corpus inscriptionum latinarum*

PGM   Hans Dieter Betz. *The Greek Magical Papyri in Translation, Including the Demotic Spells*. 2nd ed. Chicago: University of Chicago Press, 1996.

1

The Cross in Its Place

To die by crucifixion was hideous and horrific. One ancient historian called it a "most pitiable of deaths" (Josephus, *The Life* 76). One incident in particular reveals the extent to which crucifixion was recognized as a most agonizing form of torment. A Jewish soldier, captured by Roman forces in the Jewish revolt against Rome in 66–70 CE, was saved from crucifixion by the efforts of his comrades, who agreed to surrender en masse and become slaves of Rome rather than see their colleague crucified (Josephus, *Jewish War* 7.202–203). Because of the excruciating pain involved in crucifixion, one ancient rhetorician said that "the very word 'cross' should be far removed not only from the person of a Roman citizen but from his thoughts, his eyes, and his ears" (Cicero, *Pro Rabirio* 5:16). And the Jewish apostle who took the message of "Christ crucified" to the Greco-Roman world spoke of "the scandal of the cross" upon which his Lord died (Gal. 5:11; cf. 1 Cor 1:18, 23).

It is popularly imagined that, despite its scandal, early Jesus-followers were making lavish use of the sign of the cross in every place from the very start. Whereas the sign of the cross adorns the majority of churches in the Western world today, and has dominated the focus of Christian art for over a millennium, the common expectation is that the cross was at the forefront of Christian devotion and artistry since the early years of the post-Easter Jesus-movement.

A view of this kind crumbles the minute it is tested against the historical data. Although the material evidence from the early Christian centuries is relatively thin, it suggests that the cross was not at the focal point of devotion in Christian gatherings until much later. The cross came to the forefront of Christian artistic display only in the aftermath of the initiatives of Constantine, who rose to power in the early fourth century and progressively imposed Christianity and its symbols on a world he sought to unify and control.

Figure 1.1. Constantine on a Roman coin from the first half of the fourth century.

The story of the cross and Constantine goes this way. Just before entering into the Battle of the Milvian Bridge in 312, Constantine looked into the sky and saw a cross standing above the sun, together with the Greek words, "With this sign you shall conquer" (Eusebius, *Life of Constantine* 28). Because Constantine did, in fact, win the battle, this moment became a watershed in the history of Christian symbolism. It began to propel the cross (along with other Christianized symbols, especially the chi-rho symbol emblazoned on the shields of Constantine's army) to heights that it had never previously enjoyed in the artistry of Christian symbols. With a foothold in Constantine's account of his experiences prior to the Battle of the Milvian Bridge, the cross would eventually become the predominant symbol of Christianity. Embracing the symbol of the cross was further enhanced decades later when the story began to circulate that Constantine's mother, Helena, traveled to the Holy Land in 326 and found the cross of Jesus's crucifixion.[1] By the end of the century, Christian emperors such as Valentinian and his brother Valens were adopting the chi-rho as a symbol of military power and triumph—as depicted in coins showing emperors dragging a captive in their right hand (representing the subjugation of the nations) and holding a chi-rho standard in their left hand (see fig. 1.3). The symbol of the simple cross was adapted to play a significant role in the accumulation of political power.

---

1. See especially Jan W. Drijvers, *Helena Augusta: The Mother of Constantine the Great and the Legend of Her Finding of the True Cross* (Leiden: Brill, 1992).

Figure 1.2. A mid-fourth-century coin honoring Emperor Constantine II, depicting a chi-rho at the middle right.

Figure 1.3. A late fourth-century coin depicting Emperor Valens dragging by the hair a captive (i.e., the barbarian nations, on the coin's left side) through the power of the chi-rho christogram (on the coin's right side).

While this much is certainly true, one common interpretation of the material record requires adjustment. It is indisputable that the cross became a powerful symbol in the wake of Constantine's promotion of Christianity within his empire, but it is to be disputed that only in the fourth century and beyond did the cross become a Christian symbol.

In contrast to popular opinion, historians have frequently adopted the view that the cross had no place within Christian symbolism in the pre-Constantinian era. In this view, a watershed divide existed between pre- and post-Constantinian contexts, with the cross on one side but not on the other.

This view draws its impetus from the fact that there was a significant difference between the two sides of this watershed with regard to political power. Constantine gave Christianity a significant presence within political structures of power, a presence that could never have been imagined prior to Constantine's rise to power. It was only when an emperor who favored Christianity was at the helm (the argument goes) that the cross could be used for "constructive" purposes (that is, to help unify the empire). In that project, the cross became incorporated into a militaristic, triumphalist Christianity—a far cry from the humble beginnings of the early Jesus-movement nearly three hundred years earlier. Prior to the Constantinian era (the argument continues), Christians avoided the cross at all costs to ensure that their religion was not associated with the shame of crucifixion.

Something of this view was articulated by George Willard Benson long ago:

> The very fact of the cross having been used for centuries for the crucifixion of criminals was a powerful reason for not using it as a religious emblem. To the early Christians it was a symbol of disgrace. They could not look upon it as an object of reverence. Death by

crucifixion was the most shameful and ignominious that could be devised. That Christ should have been put to death, as were debased and despised criminals, was bitterly humiliating to his followers. It was years before this deep rooted feeling could be overcome.[2]

Views such as Benson's regarding Christian embarrassment about the cross of Jesus help to bolster a historical scenario in which the cross became a visual symbol only in the early fourth century and beyond, with the advent of a sociopolitical leader who actively promoted Christianity. The cross of shame was hidden and subdued by powerless Christians, who made no use of it as a symbol of devotion until such time as the cross of opportunistic and intolerant aggression emerged through the scheming initiatives of powerful Christians.

While it cannot be denied that the cross became a powerful symbol in the wake of Constantine's promotion of Christianity within his empire, subsequent chapters of this book will problematize one key component of this reconstruction—the view that only in the fourth century and beyond did the cross become a Christian symbol.

The view that the cross is absent from the material record prior to Constantine has deep roots. It is reflected, for instance, in the comments from 1875 of Pompeian archaeologist Thomas Dyer. He claimed that it is "in the highest degree improbable" that Christians would ever "have ventured to exhibit any public sign of their religion" prior to Constantine, since doing so would have jeopardized their lives.[3] More recently, Pompeian scholars have articulated much the same view, such as Agnello Baldi in 1964 and Antonio Varone in 1979. Both of them assessed material evidence with the working assumption that Christians would have done

---

2. George Willard Benson, *The Cross: Its History and Symbolism. An Account of the Symbol More Universal in Its Use and More Important in Its Significance Than Any Other in the World* (Buffalo: George Willard Benson, 1934), 28–29.

3. Thomas H. Dyer, *Pompeii: Its History, Buildings and Antiquities* (London: George Bell & Sons, 1875 [1868]), 321.

everything to avoid drawing attention to themselves prior to Constantine, from whose time the cross as a Christian symbol derives.[4]

But the view is not restricted to discourse in one scholarly corner; it is reflected far more widely by scholars of notable repute who have shaped scholarly discourse significantly. In 1951, erudite historian and archaeologist of early Christianity Erich Dinkler regarded it as "absolute dogma" that "the symbol of the cross makes its first appearance in the age of Constantine."[5] Although he would later modify this view somewhat (as we will see in chapter 5 below), it has continued in the role of "absolute dogma" since he crowned it as such. For instance, Graydon Snyder's influential work *Ante Pacem: Archaeological Evidence of Christian Life before Constantine* first appeared in 1985 but has seen reprint after reprint in the years to follow; it states simply that the cross as a symbol of Christianity "ought not be considered pre-Constantinian."[6] Snyder offers no robust engagement with the cross in the pre-Constantinian material record since, in his view, there simply is no such thing.

---

4. Agnello Baldi, *La Pompei: Giudaico-Cristiana* (Cava de Tirreni: Di Mauro Editore, 1964), 39–40; Antonio Varone, *Presenze guidaiche e cristiane a Pompei* (Naples: M. D'Auria Editore, 1979); 33.

5. Erich Dinkler, "Comments on the History of the Symbol of the Cross," *Journal for Theology and the Church* 1 (1965): 132. The article was first published in German in 1951, the quotation here being from page 157 of the 1951 article.

6. Graydon F. Snyder, *Ante pacem: Archaeological Evidence of Church Life before Constantine*, rev. ed. (Macon, GA: Mercer University Press, 2003), 14. Horn, Lieu, and Phenix cite Snyder as support when they claim that "the cross is not a significant symbol in Christian art and depiction until the fourth century" (Cornelia Horn, Samuel N. C. Lieu, and Robert R. Phenix Jr., "Beyond the Eastern Frontier," in *Early Christianity in Contexts: An Exploration across Cultures and Continents*, ed. William Tabbernee [Grand Rapids: Baker Academic, 2014], 63), but Snyder never used the important qualification "significant" that they attribute to him. Although Robin Margaret Jensen (*Understanding Early Christian Art* [New York: Routledge, 2000]) took note of the fact that a few pre-Constantinian Christian artifacts display cross-markings, her case was minimalistic and her point has not filtered into scholarly discourse: "some definite cross-markings found among the pre-Constantinian graffiti at the Vatican or on more formal Christian epitaphs elsewhere in Rome or found in other parts of the empire can be dated to the third century" (137).

With voices of repute articulating this view so unreservedly, it is little wonder that others have adopted it without restraint. In 1997, for instance, Carolyn Osiek and David Balch asserted that "the cross as a visual symbol is . . . wholly unattested for the first several Christian centuries."[7] In 2006 Mark Heim pointed his readership to what he called "the absence of images of the cross in the first four Christian centuries," claiming that there is "no entirely satisfactory explanation of why the cross would figure so centrally in Christian faith and worship, but be visually absent" from the material record.[8] And "this story is still told . . . to this day" (to hijack the claim made in Matt. 28:15).[9] My hope is that we can now begin to set the record straight and tell a story that is representative of a much fuller spread of the historical data.

What We Will and Won't Be Seeing

In the following chapters, I will propose (twisting Heim's claim around a bit) that there is no entirely satisfactory explanation as to why the material evidence of the cross in pre-Constantinian Christian circles has been neglected for so long. Prior to Constantine, the cross may not have been the object of Christian veneration that it was later to become in the fourth century and beyond; nonetheless,

---

7. Carolyn Osiek and David L. Balch, *Families in the New Testament World: Households and House Churches* (Louisville: Westminster John Knox, 1997), 86. This view receives important nuancing in David L. Balch, "The Suffering of Isis/Io and Paul's Portrait of Christ Crucified (Gal. 3:1): Frescoes in Pompeian and Roman Houses and in the Temple of Isis in Pompeii," *The Journal of Religion* 83 (2003): 53–55.

8. S. Mark Heim, "Missing the Cross? Types of the Passion in Early Christian Art," *Contagion: Journal of Violence, Mimesis, and Culture* 11–12 (2006): 183–94.

9. For instance, Oliver Larry Yarbrough ("The Shadow of an Ass: On Reading the Alexamenos Graffito," in *Text, Image, and Christians in the Graeco-Roman World*, ed. Aliou Cissé Niang and Carolyn Osiek [Eugene, OR: Pickwick, 2012], 239–54) speaks of "the absence of the crucifixion (and cross) in early Christian art" and of "Christian avoidance of the cross in art" (251). Anecdotally, I have had numerous conversations with university professors who have confessed that they have taught this view to their students for the course of their teaching career.

it was incorporated into the symbolism of the pre-Constantinian Christian imagination and found its way into the realia of the ancient world.

The view that the cross became a Christian symbol only in the fourth century has the enticing advantage of being a sleek and streamlined instrument for dissecting history into two easily managed segments, one prior to Constantine and the other in the wake of Constantine's rise to power. In subsequent chapters of this book, however, we will see evidence that overturns this attractive construct. If the cross was neither ubiquitous nor predominant in the pre-Constantinian record, neither was it absent from that record. In fact, in certain sectors it seems to have been a symbol with real attraction.

The task at hand, however, is not simply an exercise in counting artifacts. More significantly, the counted artifacts will act like windows into the character of pre-Constantinian Jesus-devotion. What those artifacts tell us about the configurations of Jesus-devotion in a pre-Constantinian environment is just as significant as the counting up of their number.

In undertaking this task, three chapters (chapters 2 through 4) clear the way for the main data that follows. Two subsequent chapters of this book bear the brunt of the weight, foregrounding the material artifacts demonstrating that the cross has a foothold within pre-Constantinian Christian devotion. The first of those chapters (chapter 5) offers an overview of the relevant material from a number of locations in the second and third centuries, while the second (chapter 6) engages one particular artifact from Pompeii, the sprawling first-century town covered by ash during the explosion of Mount Vesuvius in 79.

Much of the material evidence that will be presented in chapter 5 has already been gathered by others, but that evidence tends to be spread throughout disparate scholarly publications. This has enabled the consensus view to saunter on, since these artifacts, often from different fields of specialty, can all too easily be neglected or simply deemed to be "exceptions to the rule" and left as outliers. But when these "exceptions" are harnessed together and their full force is felt, they prove to be exceptional not only in their number but also in what they reveal about the nature of Jesus-devotion in the pre-Constantinian era.

One further chapter (chapter 7) will draw on relevant texts of the first three centuries that support the findings from the material record.[10] This will allow us ultimately to interweave the relevant textual and material records, helping us to see that what is appearing within the material record relates to what is being discussed in texts from roughly the same time and the same geographical territory. As a consequence, in chapter 8 we will plot what the extant data reveals regarding the geographical and temporal spread of Christians who made use of a cruciform symbol as an expression of their religious devotion. Unless we imagine that all the pertinent data has been salvaged from the material record without loss, the picture we can devise will have numerous holes in it. But even the tatty and threadbare tapestry that emerges enables us to recognize that the cross was, in fact, a symbol utilized by Christians long before Constantine.

---

10. It is not my intent in this project to canvass all the ancient texts pertaining to crucifixion. That hefty task has already been done by others. On crucifixion in the ancient world, see especially Martin Hengel, *Crucifixion* (Minneapolis: Fortress Press, 1977); David W. Chapman, *Ancient Jewish and Christian Perceptions of Crucifixion* (Grand Rapids: Baker Academic, 2008); John Granger Cook, "Roman Crucifixions: From the Second Punic War to Constantine," *Zeitschrift für neutestamentliche Wissenschaft* 104 (2013): 1–32; idem, *Crucifixion in the Mediterranean World* (Tübingen: Mohr Siebeck, 2014). The arguments of Gunnar Samuelsson, *Crucifixion in Antiquity: An Inquiry into the Background and Significance of the New Testament Terminology of Crucifixion* (Tübingen: Mohr Siebeck, 2013), (one of which is that the Roman cross was always only a vertical post without a crossbeam) have been compellingly dispelled by John Granger Cook, "Review of Gunnar Samuelsson's *Crucifixion in Antiquity: An Inquiry into the Background and Significance of the New Testament Terminology of Crucifixion*," *Review of Biblical Literature* (April 2014).

It is not my view that the cross was predominant among the early Christian symbols. Other symbols were also employed by pre-Constantinian Christians as symbols of faith, and some of them seem to have had a wider currency (e.g., Jesus the Good Shepherd). Moreover, the cross clearly does not have the same kind of prominence prior to Constantine that it came to have after Constantine. At that point, the cross increasingly became incorporated into Christian worship, outstripping other symbols as the preeminent symbol of the Christian faith in the centuries that followed. During the fourth through seventh centuries, the cross continued to rise to prominence as the centerpiece of Christian religious art, adorning walls and architecture at key positions in post-Constantinian places of Christian worship.[11]

Nonetheless, although the cross is neither ubiquitous nor predominant in the pre-Constantinian record of Christian symbolism, neither is it absent from that record. Artifacts from the pre-Constantinian era demonstrate that the cross was occasionally featured within the symbolism of the first three centuries of Christianity—a fact that ultimately overturns both a consensus among certain sectors of the historical disciplines and a conviction held by certain religious groups today.[12] Although the Constantinian age

11. This includes depictions of Jesus hanging on the cross. So Jensen, *Understanding Early Christian Art*, claims that "the earliest known representations of Jesus' crucifixion date to the early fifth century, and are extremely rare until the seventh" (131). See also Daryl Schmidt, "The Jesus Tradition in the Common Life of the Early Church," in *Common Life in the Early Church: Essays Honoring Graydon E. Snyder*, ed. Julian V. Hills et al. (Harrisburg, PA: Trinity Press International, 1998), 135–46. There are earlier exceptions to this rule, however, as will be shown in chapter 4.

12. Jehovah's Witnesses, for instance, have frequently made the charge that Christian denominations are idolaters who have adopted the ways of the idolater Constantine by adopting his cross as their religious symbol. So for instance, we read in one publication (*Awake!* [Nov 8, 1972], 27]): "Not until the fourth century c.e. did the cross begin coming into noticeable use among professed Christians. The one primarily responsible for this development was Emperor Constantine, a sun worshiper who is said to have accepted Christianity years before submitting to baptism while on his deathbed." This is elaborated in a later publication (*Watchtower* [May 1, 1989], 23]): "There are also inanimate objects that if venerated may lead

boosted the meteoric rise of the cross as the preeminent symbol of Christianity, it will be demonstrated within the covers of this book that much of the heavy lifting in that task had already been done for more than two centuries prior to Constantine.

Further Preliminaries

Before starting down this road toward the interpretation of ancient artifacts, several preliminary explanations are required to help the reader get around the data with relative ease. Since the reader will soon be immersed in a world of ancient artifacts, it is important to note that ancient Christian crosses often differed in their appearances. There are several primary shapes that will be important in the chapters that follow. I place them here for ease of reference, so that readers can simply turn back to this section for a quick reminder of the shapes and the names attributed to them, if necessary.

First, there is what I will call the T cross. Traditionally referred to by the Latin term *crux commissa*, the T cross has the appearance of a capital T, with the crossbar at the top of the vertical stave.

to breaking God's commandments. Among the most prominent is the cross. For centuries it has been used by people in Christendom as part of their worship. Soon God will execute his judgments against all false religions. Those who cling to them will suffer their fate." For a similar view, with venomous polemic against the "Roman" church and its infatuation with the cross, see Alexander Hislop, *The Two Babylons, or The Papal Worship Proved to be the Worship of Nimrod and His Wife* (Neptune, NJ: Loizeaux Brothers, 1916), 197–205.

Figure 1.4. A Byzantine T cross.

Second, there is what I will call the body cross (for reasons that will become evident in chapter 4). Traditionally referred to by the Latin term *crux immissa* and later known as the Latin cross, the body cross is formed with the crossbar below the top of the stave but above the middle: †.

Figure 1.5. A "body cross" on an ancient, post-Constantinian coin
from Israel.

Third, there is what I will call the equilateral cross. Traditionally referred to by the Latin term *crux quadrata*, this is a balanced cross in which all of the appendages are of roughly equal length.

Figure 1.6. An ancient ring displaying an equilateral cross.

Fourth, there is the handled cross or the Ankh (see fig. 1.7). Traditionally referred to by the Latin term *crux ansata,* this cross is formed by combining either the T cross or the body cross with a loop attached to the top, as if the cross were being carried by a piece of rope or a handle at the top. This became the established form of the Egyptian Ankh, a symbol depicting life and prosperity, and a symbol that will have a strong place in our discussion in chapter 6 below.

Figure 1.7. A stylized Egyptian Ankh, formed by placing a circular handle above a T cross.

Fifth, at times there will be discussion of a shape that was thought of as a cross in the Greco-Roman world, although twenty-first-century eyes might struggle to see it as such initially. This cross formation has traditionally been referred to by the Latin term *crux gammata* or gamma cross—named after the Greek letter gamma in its uppercase form, which looks like an upside-down L (Γ). To form a gamma cross, the gamma shape is repeated four times, with each gamma touching the others at right angles at their base, the four bases meeting at the center (see fig. 1.8). This, then, has the appearance of a swastika, an ancient symbol predating Christianity that was later used for despicable purposes in the first half of twentieth century.[13] Often the right-facing appendage (Γ) is flipped to be a left-facing appendage.

Figure 1.8. The gamma cross in both right-facing and left-facing forms. Mosaics from the marketplace in ancient Ostia.

One other cross formation will become important at key points of successive chapters—that is, the staurogram (*stauros* being Greek

---

13. For my engagement with Nazi ideology, see Bruce Longenecker, *Hitler, Jesus, and Our Common Humanity: A Jewish Survivor Interprets Life, History, and the Gospels* (Eugene, OR: Cascade, 2014).

for "cross"). The staurogram is composed by joining together the Greek letters tau (T) and rho (P), with the vertical stave of the rho superimposed upon the stave of the tau (see fig. 1.9). The combination of these two letters as a ligature predates Christian usage, but Christians adopted the tau-rho formation at a fairly early date to depict their crucified deity (see the discussions below regarding how early that date is).[14] The tau forms the shape of the cross, while the top loop of the rho sitting above the tau gives the appearance of a person's head. When used by Christians, then, the staurogram offers a visual depiction of Jesus hanging on a cross.

Figure 1.9. A staurogram, formed by superimposing a Greek rho (P) onto a Greek tau (T).

Of course, just because two intersecting lines were made on an ancient artifact does not mean that those lines represent an ancient

14. In non-Christian usage, this two-letter ligature could denote the numbers three (*trio*) or thirty (*troikas*).

Christian cross, let alone a symbol of some other kind. In the chapters pertaining to the material record, however, most of the artifacts that are discussed benefit from the fact that the crosses in them are associated with other features that derive from Christian symbolism or from other forms of Christian identification.

With these preliminaries out of the way, we can now proceed to investigate the matter at hand. Was the cross of Jesus's death a feature of Christian self-identity prior to the rise of Christianity on the world stage through the initiatives of Constantine in the early fourth century?

2

The Cross and Non-Christian Society

Wasn't it the case that Christians before Constantine wanted to keep a low profile for fear of being spotted for their faith? And in that effort to keep a low profile, wasn't it the case that adopting the cross as a symbol of their religious devotion would only have added risk to their already precarious lives? And, moreover, shouldn't it be the case that if we find any cross within the material record prior to Constantine, it should be interpreted without reference to Christianity? Before turning to the material record, we need first to consider whether such questions regarding Christians and their places within pre-Constantinian societies have the force that they sometimes have been afforded.

Persecutions and Contexts

The common view builds on the notion that Christians were wary of letting their religious commitment become public. We can imagine this in caricatured fashion, with fear of the persecuting authorities causing Christians to have huddled together in small enclaves, where they kept to themselves and tried not to draw attention to themselves. In one caricature, for instance, the underground catacombs of Rome might be depicted as places where Christians hid away in secret, duping all others as to their whereabouts, thereby saving their skin from the barbarous pagans who strode confidently above ground, seeking to kill them all. This scenario has no advocates in serious historical scholarship. Whatever else the catacombs might have been, they were not secret hovels of protection for fearful Christians.[1]

Nonetheless, it is true that Christians were often at the receiving end of persecution. There may be a case for differentiating between "soft persecution" (i.e., social ostracism) and "hard persecution" (i.e., individuals losing their lives for their devotion to Jesus), but even so, both forms of persecution have strong footholds within the experiences of pre-Constantinian Christians. Moreover, what began as soft persecution may well have developed into hard persecution in some cases.

There are notable incidents of hard persecution in the earliest days of Christianity. These include the martyrdoms of Stephen in the early 30s (Acts 6:8–8:4, a martyrdom that the author links to a "severe persecution" against the church in Jerusalem), James the brother of John in the early 40s (Acts 12:1–2), and Antipas sometime prior to 95 (Rev. 2:13). Further, James the brother of Jesus, who had long been recognized as the head of Jerusalem Jesus-groups, was killed in 62 by the high priest Ananas (Josephus, *Jewish Antiquities* 20.197–203), a killing that was probably motivated at least in part by his devotion to Jesus. Moreover, after three of Rome's fourteen sections were burned by fires on July 18 in the year 64, the emperor Nero began a campaign against his chosen scapegoats, the "Christians" of Rome,

---

1. So Robert Speaight, "Review of F. van der Meer, *Early Christian Art* (London: Faber, 1969)," *Journal of the Royal Society of Arts* 117 (1969): 295: "The catacombs were cemeteries; they were not the deliberate creations of clandestine."

who were torn apart by wild animals, burned at the stake, brutalized in the most atrocious ways.[2] Correspondence between Pliny the Younger and the emperor Trajan (*Epistulae* 10.96–97, dated to 112) demonstrates that Christians were being executed for their loyalty to Jesus, although not through state-sanctioned pogroms.

Similar cases of hard persecution are replicated in later times as well. Here, special mention goes to the martyrs of the late second and early third centuries—including people mentioned by name by Tertullian (i.e., Mucius, Empedocles, Regulus, Anaxarchus, Zeno, and others).[3] Half a century later the emperor Decius declared that all people were required to make sacrifices to the traditional deities; although Decius's edict was not specifically an anti-Christian pogrom, Christians nonetheless became targeted, often with tragic outcomes, albeit for a period of less than two years. Then again, the Great Persecution of Diocletian in 303 reintroduced the same pressures on Christians, often with the same dire results, for just under a decade.

These are some of the horrendous moments in the history of early Christianity. But it is also important to notice that many of these instances were relatively short-lived events, and some were quite localized. In fact, there are notable stretches of time when spikes of hard persecution are absent. The sporadic martyrdoms of a few Jerusalem-based Jesus-followers in the 30s and 40s did not

---

2. These are events that the New Testament Gospels might be referring to when they discuss families being torn in two by the pressures of persecution; see Matt. 10:17–21; 24:9–14; Mark 13:9–13; Luke 21:12–19.

3. See Tertullian, *Apologies* 50. The martyrologies of the second and third centuries have recently been accused of having been sensationalistically exaggerated. See Candida R. Moss, *The Myth of Persecution: How Early Christians Invented a Story of Martyrdom* (New York: HarperOne, 2013), whose case is an important corrective to certain uses of martyrologies, although it is not without problems of its own; see for instance N. Clayton Croy, "Review of Candida R. Moss, *The Myth of Persecution*," *Review of Biblical Literature* (October 2013). A different approach to that of Moss appears in Bryan M. Litfin, *Early Christian Martyr Stories: An Evangelical Introduction with New Translations* (Grand Rapids: Baker Academic, 2014).

deter some in the 50s with "middling" status in pro-Roman Corinth from reconfiguring their religious devotion in relation to the deity who had been crucified on a Roman cross.[4] Furthermore, the two decades immediately following Nero's persecution were a notably quiet time in the register of hard persecution against Christians. Nero's horrendous persecution against Christians in Rome may, in fact, have inspired a quiet sympathy or respect for Christians among the general populace—or so Tacitus suggests when he writes of Nero's pogroms against Christians (*Annals* 15.44.5): "Hence compassion began to arise [*miseratio oriebatur*] (although toward a people who were guilty and deserving of the most unusual exemplary punishments), as if they were being eliminated not for the public utility but for the savagery of one man."

Something similar is recorded as having happened in Tertullian's day, with persecution having captured people's interest to the extent that some decided to convert to Christianity as a consequence of their consideration of the Christian message.[5] Evidently, then, we must be cautious against allowing history to be written simply by the powerful. It was not always the case that the Neros of this world saw things in the same way as the many "commoners" whom they governed.

Hard persecution against Christians in the pre-Constantinian period was not ubiquitous; instead, it was concentrated in certain times and places, with large temporal and spatial gaps between those instances. For example, in the period between the emperorships of Decius and Diocletian, the emperor Gallienus (sole emperor from

---

4. On the "middling" economic status of certain Corinthian Jesus-followers, see Bruce Longenecker, *Remember the Poor: Paul, Poverty, and the Greco-Roman World* (Grand Rapids: Eerdmans, 2010), 220–53; Timothy A. Brookins, *Corinthian Wisdom, Stoic Philosophy, and the Ancient Economy* (Cambridge: Cambridge University Press, 2014), 104–24.

5. Jane Merdinger, "Roman North Africa," in *Early Christianity in Contexts: An Exploration across Cultures and Continents*, ed. William Tabbernee (Grand Rapids: Baker Academic, 2014), 237. Tertullian himself seems to have been converted in this fashion.

260–268) issued an official edict extending tolerance toward Christians. Earlier, Tertullian recounts incidents in which proconsuls released Christians from imprisonment, demonstrating that "some Roman officials harbored no ill will against Christians and were reluctant to convict them."[6] Moreover, a significant proportion of inscriptions from the Carsamba Valley (bordering Lycaonia) "demonstrates an unusually high degree of toleration for Christianity by local officials" in the third century.[7] Elsewhere, several Christians in the last quarter of the third century had their self-portraits engraved within rings that declared them to be the property "of Jesus Christ" or "of Christ."[8]

Further, in the cities and towns of the Upper Tembris Valley in Phrygia, a number of third-century inscriptions adorning tombs include the phrase "Christians for Christians" alongside the names of those entombed and those still living who erected the tombs on their behalf.[9] These tomb inscriptions recorded information that was evidently well known regarding the identity of local Christians. That Christians would identify themselves as such on public monuments testifies "to the peaceful cohabitation of pagans and Christians in that part of Phrygia."[10] As W. M. Calder argued in the mid-twentieth century, these inscriptions offer us "a picture of Christian well-being" that was "not seriously disturbed by occasional official persecutions,

6. Ibid.

7. William Tabbernee, "Asia Minor and Cyprus," in *Early Christianity in Contexts*, 316.

8. See Jeffrey Spier, *Late Antique and Early Christian Gems* (Wiesenbaden: Reichert, 2007), 18, with plates 2 and 3; see also page 30 with plate 103.

9. See William Tabbernee, *Montanist Inscriptions and Testimonia: Epigraphic Sources Illustrating the History of Montanism* (Macon, GA: Mercer University Press, 1997), 24, 25, 27–29, 31, 38–52.

10. Tabbernee, "Asia Minor and Cyprus," 316. See also the inscription on the lid of a sarcophagus dated to the time between 212 and 248. The inscription reads: "Aurelios Gaios son of Apphianus, a Christian, prepared [this sarcophagus] for himself and for Aurelia Stratoneikiane his wife, being herself a Christian." See Tabbernee, *Montanist Inscriptions and Testimonia*, 13; Tabbernee, "Asia Minor and Cyprus," 289.

some of them half-hearted, and more frequent popular pogroms."[11] The same point has been made more recently by Jane Merdinger:

> [These inscriptions are] indicative of a sense of security engendered by the tolerant attitude toward Christians and Christianity by the non-Christian inhabitants of West-Central Phrygia. Christianity, it appears, was not deemed to be an especially serious threat to the native Phrygian cults and the cults brought into Phrygia from elsewhere, at least not in the first three centuries of Christian presence in the area.[12]

This helps to explain the notable rise of Christianity within the same geographical area. William Tabbernee has recently stated that prior to the year 250

> Christians in Phrygia rarely had to prove their loyalty publicly, and . . . until the so-called Great Persecution (303–313), there was little implementation of imperial anti-Christian legislation in the area. Consequently, Christianity in Phrygia was relatively free to make converts and to establish Christian communities. By the beginning of the fourth century, some of these communities had grown so significantly that, reportedly, the majority of the population in particular towns was Christian.[13]

Moreover, as Tabbernee notes, within certain sectors of Asia Minor in particular, urban councilors and senators included a "surprisingly large number of Christians" by the mid-third century; by then, "people of high social status had become Christians . . . [who] could, theoretically at least, have exerted considerable political influence on behalf of Christianity." Little wonder, then, that "by the beginning of the fourth century, some cities in Phrygia had declared themselves to be predominantly (if not totally) Christian."[14]

---

11. William M. Calder, "Early-Christian Epitaphs from Phrygia," *Anatolian Studies* 5 (1955): 27. See also idem, "Philadelphia and Montanism," *Bulletin of the John Rylands Library* 7 (1922–23): 309.

12. Merdinger, "Roman North Africa," 237. It was once thought that these must have been Montanist Christians; against that view, see footnote 71 in chapter 5 below.

13. Tabbernee, "Asia Minor and Cyprus," 272.

In light of these and other indicators, one searches high and low for a long-term, empire-wide pogrom against Christians in the pre-Constantinian age. If anything, when the full sweep of the first three centuries is kept in view, hard persecution seems to have been more the exception than the rule.[15]

This does not mean, of course, that adopting Christian devotion was an uncomplicated prospect outside those situations. Christians were often recipients of low-grade forms of social alienation, sometimes leading to notable personal misfortune (cf. Mark 13; Heb. 10:32–34; 1 Pet. 3:16–17; see also Acts 4:1–22; 5:17–42; 12:6–11; etc.). The fact that hard persecution had flared up against Jesus-followers at times during the very earliest days of the Jesus-movement would have fostered an air of attentive caution and guarded vigilance among Christians in many locations. Caution must have been the order of the day for many of them.

Much more could be said regarding the complex and diverse postures taken by Christians in the pre-Constantinian period.[16] But what is impressive are those moments in the pre-Constantinian era when Christians seem not to have been too concerned about hiding their religious identity, despite the attentive caution they must nonetheless have exhibited. Christians to whom 1 Peter was

14. Ibid., 317; compare ibid., 318, where the same is said of Cyprus. See especially Jan Nicolaas Bremmer, "*Christianus sum*: The Early Christian Martyrs and Christ," in *Eulogia: Mélanges offerts à Antoon A. R. Bastiaensen*, ed. G. J. M. Bartelink, A. Hilhorst, and C. H. Kneepkens (The Hague: Nijhoff International, 1991), 11–20.

15. Bart D. Ehrman (*Lost Christianities* [New York: Oxford University Press, 2003], 344) speaks of persecutions against Christians as being "relatively infrequent and sporadic," wrongly adding (not least in the case of Nero and Decius) that "they were never promoted from the highest levels, the imperial government." Better is Everett Ferguson (*Church History* [Grand Rapids: Zondervan, 2005], 70): "Before Marcus Aurelius, action against Christians was limited because their numbers seemed few. Since only the governor could pronounce the death sentence, most of the known cases of martyrdom were in the great provincial cities. Governors were allowed a wide latitude by Roman law. The threat of persecution was ever present, but it was not a constant experience."

16. On this, see especially Lucy Grig, *Making Martyrs in Late Antiquity* (London: Duckworth, 2004).

addressed, for instance, clearly were somewhere on the scale of soft-to-hard persecution, and yet the Petrine author unfailingly exhorts his readers to live lives that unashamedly contribute to the betterment of society, and to do so to the credit of Jesus Christ. They were repeatedly exhorted in this fashion (1 Pet. 3:16–17; cf. 2:12, 20; 3:11; 4:19): "Keep your conscience clear, so that, when you are maligned, those who abuse you for your good conduct in Christ may be put to shame. For it is better to suffer for doing good, if suffering should be God's will, than to suffer for doing evil."

The Petrine author seems to imagine that persecuted Christians are actively promoting good within society in some fashion, conceiving of their identity as one of "soft difference" or "holy engagement" (as some scholars have labeled it) and expecting that Jesus-groups might gain respect within their cultural context.[17] The Petrine author calls Christians to be a "blessing" within their indigenous contexts (3:9), so that they actively seek the welfare of their neighbors.[18] If Christians had already experienced persecution in some form, the Petrine author does not imagine his Christian audience to be hiding away in safe hovels far from the madding crowd.

The view of the Petrine author is much like that of another from the late first century or early second century. The author of 1 Timothy urges that Christians pray for everyone, including people in high positions, "so that we may lead a quiet and peaceable life in all

---

17. See, for instance, Miroslav Volf, "Soft Difference: Theological Reflections on the Relation between Church and Culture in 1 Peter," *Ex Auditu* 10 (1994): 15–30; Joel B. Green, "Identity and Engagement in a Diverse World: Pluralism and Holiness in 1 Peter," *Asbury Theological Journal* 55 (2010): 85–92.

18. So Reinhard Feldmeier, *The First Letter of Peter* (Waco, TX: Baylor University Press, 2008), 186; cf. David M. Shaw, "Called to Bless: Considering an Under-appreciated Aspect of 'Doing Good' in 1 Peter," paper presented to the Social World of the New Testament Seminar of the British New Testament Conference, Manchester, UK, 2014. This may not have involved public benefaction, as some have suggested; on this issue, see especially Travis Williams, *Good Works in 1 Peter: Negotiating Social Conflict and Christian Identity in the Greco-Roman World* (Tübingen: Mohr Siebeck, 2014).

godliness and dignity" (2:1–2). This vision is not motivated by fear as much as by prudent caution.

A century or so after these biblical authors, Tertullian offers a similar picture. He outlines the kind of soft persecution that Christians may have experienced with some frequency (*Apology* 3):

> What are we to think of it, that most people so blindly knock their heads against the hatred of the Christian name; that when they bear favorable testimony to any one, they mingle with it abuse of the name he bears? "A good man," says one, "is Gaius Seius, only that he is a Christian." So another, "I am astonished that a wise man like Lucius should have suddenly become a Christian."[19]

Here, although freemen or freedmen of good reputation find their status made vulnerable by their advocacy of Jesus-devotion, they have not gone into hiding, preventing others from knowing of their Christian faith for fear of being burned at the stake.[20] Their faith had become known in the public arena, where they encountered nothing more than low-grade forms of social ostracism.

This plays directly into another text from Tertullian, and one in which the cross itself is mentioned. Although Christians underwent times of persecution to one degree or another at various times in the first three centuries, that did not deter Tertullian from talking about the sign of the cross as a means of public proclamation (*Against Marcion* 3.22). Echoing several psalms of the Old Testament, Tertullian claimed that Christian symbols and practices "ascribe glory to God the Father, in the person of Christ Himself" resulting in praise of God "in the congregations" so that his "name shall be great

---

19. Tertullian continues in apologetic mode: "Nobody thinks it needful to consider whether Gaius is not good and Lucius wise, on this very account that he is a Christian; or a Christian, for the reason that he is wise and good. They praise what they know, they abuse what they are ignorant of, and they inspire their knowledge with their ignorance."

20. Moreover, they bear the names of either freedmen, in which case they were Roman citizens on earning their manumission, or freemen, in which case they probably inherited Roman citizenship at birth. These are not slaves.

among the Gentiles." In that same passage, Tertullian lists some of the Christian practices that glorify God, including "the sign upon the forehead, the sacraments of the church, and the offerings of the pure sacrifice." This "sign upon the forehead" is almost certainly the cross. And with these glorifying practices, Christians "ought now to burst forth, and declare that the Spirit of the Creator prophesied of your Christ." There is nothing here about hiding the cross away as a symbol of embarrassment and dishonor; precisely the opposite is the case. The sign of the cross is one of the articles of Christian identity that enhances the glory of God among the nations, as Christians publicly declare their worship of God. Tertullian's rhetoric might be overblown, and his target audience may be solely Christian, but the attitude and posture he adopts do not correspond to fear and trembling.

We see much the same in Tertullian's contemporary, Clement of Alexandria (c. 150–215). Although much of his life is lost to us, it seems that he converted to Christianity after having studied Greek philosophy and immersing himself in the mystery religions of his day and in Jewish theology. In his writings, he commends Christianity to non-Christians (i.e., his *Exhortation to the Greeks,* written in the mid-190s) and instructs Christians in ethical reasoning (i.e., his *Christ the Educator,* written in the late 190s). This is how G. W. Butterworth describes Clement's significance in the context of the late second century:[21]

> In the second century Christianity had become a power. No longer was the Church weak, poor and neglected. Educated men inquired about its faith, and asked admittance within its fold; but they would bring with them an inheritance of thought and culture, unknown to the simple Christians of an earlier age. The question was bound to arise, What

21. G. W. Butterworth, *Clement of Alexandria,* Loeb 92 (New York: G. P. Putnam's Sons, 1919), xiv.

relation has this [inheritance] to the Christian faith? Is it to be set aside as superfluous, or injurious? Or is all the good in it to be accepted and welcomed, a proof that God's revelation extends in a measure to all men, to Greeks as well as Jews? Clement himself had come to Christianity with a mind steeped in Greek learning, and he answered this question with clearness and confidence.

We would be wrong, then, to characterize Christian devotion in the late second century as necessarily a fragile and introverted phenomenon; instead, in some respects it was a powerful force within Greco-Roman culture that even some "educated men inquired about."

With Justin Martyr, Clement of Alexandria, Tertullian, and various others, the second century had its fair share of theologians engaging in apologetics in an effort to make the Christian faith understandable to outsiders.[22] While their texts were usually written for the benefit of other Christians, they were intended to educate Christians in how to engage non-Christians in discourse about their faith—a posture that does not coincide well with a caricature of Christians hiding behind locked doors.[23]

All of this coheres with recent advances in conceptualizing the worship settings of pre-Constantinian Christianity. Scholars have tended to use "the house church" as the default for modeling the worship settings of early Christians, with Christians gathering quietly

---

22. And here we recall Robert Louis Wilken's important point (*The Christians as the Romans Saw Them* [New Haven, CT: Yale University Press, 1984], esp. 197–205) that Christian theology benefited from the critiques of its critics during the first centuries of Christian theological reflection.

23. Larry Hurtado has made the point this way: "When you have spokesmen for a religious movement framing formal defenses of it ('*apologia*') and addressing these to the Emperor (e.g., Justin Martyr) and to the wider public (e.g., Epistle to Diognetus), I'd say that's hardly trying to remain under cover! That's not simply putting your head 'above the parapet,' that's standing up on top of the parapet and waving your arms!" See his blog post titled "Was Early Christianity Secretive?" *Larry Hurtado's Blog*, July 30, 2014, http://larryhurtado.wordpress.com/2014/07/30/was-early-christianity-secretive-2/. Much the same point was made by the Lukan evangelist when writing the following: "There were many lamps in the room upstairs where we were meeting" (Acts 20:8); "this was not done in a corner" (Acts 26:26).

and unnoticed behind the secured doors of a private house.[24] The past two decades have seen the viability of this model eroded somewhat. Investigations of "houses and society" in Pompeii and Herculaneum, for instance, have problematized the applicability of the adjective "private" in relation to the variety of residences in these two Vesuvian towns. Demarcating Greco-Roman residences as private space fails to account for the influx of public availability and usage that characterized a broad spectrum of Vesuvian residences.[25]

For this reason, Andrew Wallace-Hadrill has effectively proposed that we shift our language from "house" or "household" to "houseful" when describing many Greco-Roman residences, with "houseful" being understood as "a group unconnected in family terms except by coresidence."[26] To give just one example, residences in Pompeii and Herculaneum often had upper-story apartments that were accessed by tenants through a stairway in a main residence (e.g., Herculaneum's House of the Bicentenary). If a group of Christians were worshiping in the alae of a residence, they would have been seen and heard by tenants entering or exiting those apartments.

If we are to imagine pre-Constantinian Christians meeting in residential space, we must also allow for the fact that those spaces were often exposed to others beyond the participants in worship. It is not at all obvious that Christians could have hoped to keep their devotion hidden from view. In many instances, there were too many

---

24. An example of this from Judea might be Acts 12:12–17.

25. See, for instance, Andrew Wallace-Hadrill, "*Domus* and *Insulae* in Rome: Families and Housefuls," in *Early Christian Families in Context: An Interdisciplinary Dialogue*, ed. David L. Balch and Carolyn Osiek (Grand Rapids: Eerdmans, 2003), 3–18; idem, *Houses and Society in Pompeii and Herculaneum* (Princeton, NJ: Princeton University Press, 1994). He is followed by Carolyn Osiek and David L. Balch, *Families in the New Testament World: Households and House Churches* (Louisville: Westminster John Knox, 1997), 24–25; David L. Balch, "Rich Pompeian Houses, Shops for Rent, and the Huge Apartment Building as Typical Spaces for Pauline House Churches," *Journal for the Study of the New Testament* 27 (2004): 28–29.

26. Wallace-Hadrill, *Houses and Society in Pompeii and Herculaneum*, 92.

moving parts in the relationship between a residence and broader society for such a hope to have been realistic.

It is these "moving parts" that the apostle Paul is probably referring to when he mentions the prospect of "outsiders or unbelievers" observing what goes on in Christian worship (1 Cor. 14:23–24)—almost as if those "outsiders" simply happened to walk in on the worship proceedings. This passage seems to illustrate that a "house church" setting did not inevitably enable Christians to shelter away in the safety of isolated seclusion; the convenience of that heuristic model is problematized by the complexity of residential space in the archaeological record.

Moreover, scholars are increasingly taking account of other settings in which Christians were known to have worshiped.[27] Beyond "the house church," pre-Constantinian Christians were known to have assembled in a variety of settings, such as shops, workshops, barns, warehouses, inns, rented dining rooms, bathhouses, gardens, waterside spaces, open urban spaces, and burial sites. Edward Adams's recent study of these settings demonstrates that many of the settings involved a "public" dimension in one way or another.[28] Even the mere practicalities of prearranging and performing corporate worship (for instance, in rented dining facilities) diminished the prospects that Christians could have been "secretive" in their aspirations. This is not to deny that Christians

---

27. See, for instance, David G. Horrell, "Domestic Space and Christian Meetings at Corinth: Imagining New Contexts and the Building East of the Theatre," *New Testament Studies* 50 (2004): 349–69; Balch, "Rich Pompeian Houses"; and especially Robert Jewett, *Romans: A Commentary* (Minneapolis: Fortress Press, 2006), 62–69.

28. Edward Adams, *The Earliest Christian Meeting Places: Almost Exclusively Houses?* (New York: Bloomsbury T & T Clark, 2013). Of outdoor spaces, for instance, Adams has this to say: "It would surely have been possible for a Christian teacher to sit in the street, on a street corner, or at the corner of the marketplace with a small group of disciples" (191–92). Adams then notes the attraction of such outdoor locations as offering "a better opportunity for recruitment," since "giving Christian instruction to insiders in public places where outsiders would also be present would [have] been an indirect . . . way of proselytizing." There is nothing in his model about Christians fearfully hiding their faith from others.

often would have found ways to engage in secretive worship; in many settings, however, the realities involved meant that Christian worship would have been recognizable to others.

One final observation needs also to be registered. That is, what motivated soft and hard forms of persecution against Christians was not primarily their worship of a deity who had been crucified. What bothered most opponents of Christianity was the failure of Christians to bolster central pillars of Greco-Roman life—not least, worship of non-Christian deities and the emperor. If Christians had been successful in finding ways to include worship of the emperor within their Jesus-devotion, a crucified deity might have been a curious oddity to most non-Christians, but it would not have been a central point of animosity. It really is not correct to say, then, that Christians "were persecuted simply because they chose to worship Christ."[29] More precisely, the persecuted among the Christians were those who chose not to worship other deities.[30]

---

29. Osiek and Balch, *Families in the New Testament World*, 185.

30. I need to register my understanding of the word "deity" when used of Jesus Christ in the first-century Mediterranean context. I understand the early Jesus–movement to have included what is traditionally termed a "high Christology" in which Jesus was heralded from a very early date as included within the divine identity—sometime in the 30s. Originally his place within the divine identity was conceived within the cradle of Jewish monotheistic theology, in which Jesus was in some fashion understood to be an expression of the almighty deity worshiped within Judaism—a "mutation" of traditional Jewish devotion. On this fascinating subject, see Larry Hurtado, *One God, One Lord: Early Christian Devotion and Ancient Jewish Monotheism* (Minneapolis: Fortress Press, 1988); idem, *Lord Jesus Christ: Devotion to Jesus in Earliest Christianity* (Grand Rapids: Eerdmans, 2005); Richard Bauckham, *Jesus and the God of Israel: God Crucified and Other Studies on the New Testament's Christology of Divine Identity* (Grand Rapids: Eerdmans, 2008); Daniel Boyarin, *The Jewish Gospels: The Story of the Jewish Christ* (New York: The New Press, 2011); Andrew Chester, "High Christology—When, When, and Why?" *Early Christianity* 2 (2011): 22–50; N. T. Wright, *Paul and the Faithfulness of God* (Minneapolis: Fortress Press, 2013), 644–56. I imagine, however, that the theological nuances of Jewish monotheistic devotion were frequently lost in the transmission of Jesus-devotion within the first-century Greco-Roman world. We must assume that the rich Jewish theological nuances of someone like the apostle Paul would have been retained with varying degrees of success in different contexts of the Greco-Roman world. For many ordinary devotees of Jesus across the Mediterranean basin, the divinity of Jesus Christ may have been unadorned by the full nuancing of Judeo-Christian theologizing about how that pertains to the almighty creator who had covenanted himself to Israel. So, for instance, the second-century

This is not to say, of course, that the cross had no part in anti-Christian slurs. Clearly it did. For instance, in the mid-second century Justin Martyr recognized that non-Christians considered Christian suffering to arise from the madness of putting "a crucified man in second place after the unchangeable and eternal God" (*First Apology* 1.13.4). In the mid-third century, the Alexandrian theologian Origen registered the depiction of Christianity offered by Celsus, his long-departed rhetorical opponent, who had decried Christianity as the worship of a man who "was nailed to a cross" (*Contra Celsum* 6.34). But these criticisms of the cross seem to have been taunting gibes that attached themselves to much more substantial critiques of Jesus-devotion. At best, mocking the crucified deity was a derivative form of derision, not a central focus of antagonism. As such, we should be wary of imagining that belittling Christianity for its devotion to a crucified deity was a ubiquitous focal point in the criticism of Christianity in all of its pre-Constantinian settings.

But even if it could be shown that mockery of the Christians' crucified deity was ubiquitous within the pre-Constantinian centuries of the Common Era, that does not mean that the cross could never have served as a symbol of Christian devotion within that time frame. Perhaps it served in that role *despite* the ubiquitous criticism. Or perhaps the ubiquitous criticism arose *as a consequence* of the incorporation of the cross as a symbol within Jesus-devotion. In any of these scenarios, "fear of persecution" falls away as an adequate support to the view that the cross could not have served as a Christian symbol at any point prior to Constantine.

---

rhetor Lucian referred to Christians as having brought a new cult into the world (*Peregrinus* 11)—evidently without cognizance of the Jewish context out of which it had emerged. On this, see also M. David Litwa, *Iesus Deus: The Early Christian Depiction of Jesus as a Mediterranean God* (Minneapolis: Fortress Press, 2014).

The Relevance of "Christianities"

There is another reason for questioning the basis for the standard explanation regarding the alleged absence of the cross in pre-Constantinian Christian symbolism. As some scholars are eager to point out, Christianity was hardly a monolithic block in the pre-Constantinian period. "Christianities" were spread across a fairly wide taxonomy of convictions, commitments, and practices. Diversity ranged within and between proto-orthodox and gnostic forms of Christianities. Historians and theologians have tended to abandon the terms "orthodox" and "heresy" when studying the first three centuries of the Christian era, precisely because history is far messier than such lazy classifications allow. Early Christian identity cannot be packaged up within neatly organized boxes with conveniently simplistic labels attached to them. Scholars in the late twentieth century and beyond have repeatedly demonstrated that Christianity in the first centuries of the Common Era was "neither chronologically predictable nor theologically consistent."[31]

Although this "varieties of Jesus" approach can be taken too far, it nonetheless has substantial merit and problematizes attempts to say what characterized "all Christianities" (or "every form of Christianity") during the pre-Constantinian period. To say that pre-Constantinian Christianity was characterized by variety and difference makes it difficult to say in the same breath that the cross had no pre-Constantinian presence within the variety of Christianities, or even that it never arose as a symbol within an anomalous or singularly indigenous form of Christianity.

---

31. This is the publisher's website marketing blurb for Tabbernee, *Early Christianity in Contexts*. On this issue in general, see Ehrman, *Lost Christianities*. The roots of this view are quite well established, going back to Walter Bauer, *Rechtgläubigkeit und Ketzerei im ältesten Christentum* (Tübingen: J. C. B. Mohr, 1934; this work was translated as *Orthodoxy and Heresy in Earliest Christianity* by Robert Kraft [Philadelphia: Fortress Press, 1971]).

One factor in which this is especially true was the potential assimilation of the polytheistic tendencies within certain forms of pre-Constantinian devotion to Jesus Christ. The consensus view seems to be built on the assumption that Christians were uniformly exclusivist in their devotion to a single deity, so a cross would automatically advertise Christians as "atheists" to their contemporaries, consequently endangering them. No doubt there were times and occasions when things lined up along this axis, and such moments are heralded in the Christian martyrologies of the second and third centuries.[32] But there are other options for Christian devotion within the ancient world. A taxonomy of Christianities from pure exclusivism to pure syncretism has a hundred and one variations within it. The appearance of a Christian cross on a third-century ring, for instance, may not tell us anything about whether the ring wearer worshiped Jesus exclusively (monotheism), or primarily but not exclusively (henotheism), or simply as one of many deities (polytheism).[33] There might well have been people who self-identified as Christians but who avoided forms of persecution (whether "soft" or "hard") because their devotion to a crucified-but-risen deity was not constructed in exclusivist frames of reference. In instances of that sort, wearing a ring with a cross on it might have induced no real detrimental effects. The issue of Christian identity in non-Christian culture is problematized further, then, once variety in Christian devotion is factored into our modeling of the pre-Constantinian world (just as in the post-Constantinian world).

---

32. Candida R. Moss proposes that "the majority of extant martyr acts date from the Decian period and beyond" (*Ancient Christian Martyrdom: Diverse Practices, Theologies, and Traditions* [New Haven, CT: Yale University Press, 2012], 166). If she is right, the implications for our reconstruction of our understanding of pre-Constantinian Christianities are even more pressing.
33. On henotheism, see especially Stephen Mitchell, *Anatolia: Land, Men, and Gods in Asia Minor* (Oxford: Clarendon, 1993), 2:43–50.

One example from the New Testament illustrates the point. Although the Johannine Apocalypse notes one instance of martyrdom among the Christians it addresses (Rev. 2:13, as noted above), the author was more concerned about the number of Jesus-followers who saw their devotion to the resurrected deity as compatible with standard forms of Greco-Roman religious practice. For those who adopted the views of "the Nicolaitans" and of "Jezebel," for instance, Jesus-devotion did not purge all other religious commitments (Rev 2:14–16, 20–23; cf. 3:15–18).[34] Their contemporaries might have considered devotion to a crucified deity to be an oddity, but there would have been no reason to persecute those Jesus-followers who fitted comfortably within standard religious configurations of the Greco-Roman world—such as those Christians who could comfortably say, "I am rich, I have prospered, and I need nothing" (3:17).

Scenarios of this kind suggest that when an ethos of persecution is prioritized, certain forms of legitimate inquiry are inevitably diminished. Painting the pre-Constantinian era with a broad brush that accentuates the colors of persecution can desensitize us to the rich varieties of tint, shade, and pigment within the diverse historical canvas.

There is, then, plenty of scope for asking the kind of questions that Warren Carter lists as profitable for pursuit of the bigger picture of Christian experiences within the pre-Constantinian period: "How did Romans regard Christians who were culturally very accommodated? How did Romans engage Christians in everyday

34. Richard B. Hays, *The Moral Vision of the New Testament: A Contemporary Introduction to New Testament Ethics* (San Francisco: HarperOne, 1996), 170, 177: "the churches were threatened less by organized oppression than by comfortable complacency. . . . Those who advocate eating idol-food apparently think they can blend in as 'normal' members of their society; perhaps some even argue that Christians can accommodate the emperor cult as a civic obligation without betraying their faith in Jesus."

life and work, in trades and entertainments, in neighborhoods and households, in civic celebrations and food insecurity?" Carter proposes that "urgent and central investigation" into early forms of Christianity should concentrate on "decentering persecution . . . and investigating the everyday 'norms' and forms of interaction from which 'persecution' was an occasional departure. How did 'Romans' and 'Christians' interact in the vast space 'in between' the persecutions?"[35]

Clearly, the persecution of Christians cannot be annexed from the inventories of Christian experience in the pre-Constantinian world. It is less clear, however, that persecution should be allowed to steamroll the terrain of inquiry, flattening the contours of early Christian experience and precluding the possibility of certain options. In this regard, and beyond the legitimate points of inquiry highlighted by Carter, one other simple question arises: Was there any space within the diversity of pre-Constantinian Christianity for the cross to take hold as a symbol of Jesus-devotion?

Reconfiguring Values

The study of survival strategies among disempowered groups reveals the way in which disenfranchised groups frequently fill powerful symbols with fresh meanings and valences. Symbols are highly malleable and open to diverse interpretations through reconfiguration of their symbolic valuation. So, for instance, as social-scientific studies have repeatedly demonstrated, despised groups readily transform labels of debasement used against them into labels they subsequently accept and flaunt for themselves—as if to snub those intent on demeaning their group identity. The terms

---

35. Warren Carter, "Review of John Granger Cook, *Roman Attitudes Toward the Christians: From Claudius to Hadrian.* Tübingen: Mohr Siebeck: 2010," *Review of Biblical Literature* (June 2014), http://www.bookreviews.org/pdf/8676_9535.pdf.

outsiders use to deride a disempowered group are often inverted by members of that group, who revalue those terms and transform "the values assigned to [them by outsiders], so that comparisons which were previously negative are now perceived as positive."[36]

So, for instance, in the Civil Rights movement of the 1960s and '70s, the adjective "black" was stripped of its derogatory sense and revitalized as a term of individual and corporate pride. Similarly, it was once demeaning to refer to a homosexual as "queer"; now, however, the term has been reconstructed as a term positively denoting homosexual identity. And as David Horrell has recently demonstrated, in the first century the very term "Christian" was itself "transformed from a hostile label applied by outsiders to a proudly claimed self-designation."[37]

Precisely this kind of revaluation is what we see in the earliest decades of the Jesus-movement with regard to the cross. Here we must initially foreground the apostle Paul, who was one of the first to give the cross a theological makeover. Although he recognized that the cross is "foolishness to gentiles," he nonetheless placed "Christ crucified" front and center in his public proclamation (1 Cor. 1:23; compare 1:18), deciding "to know nothing among you except Jesus Christ, and him crucified" (1 Cor. 2:2). Consequently, when some people challenged Paul, he characterized them not in terms of their opposition to him but as "enemies of the cross of Christ" (Phil. 3:18).

---

36. Henri Tajfel and John Turner, "An Integrative Theory of Intergroup Conflict," in *Intergroup Relations: Essential Readings*, ed. Michael A. Hogg and Dominic Abrams (Philadelphia: Psychology Press, 2001), 104.

37. David G. Horrell, "The Label Χριστιανός: 1 Peter 4:16 and the Formation of Christian Identity," *Journal of Biblical Literature* 126 (2007): 362. I am not as convinced as he is, however, that the term "Christian" has its origins in an agonistic context, or that agonistic contexts were quite as widespread as he suggests. His emphases are shared by his student, Travis Williams (see Travis Williams, *Persecution in 1 Peter: Differentiating and Contextualizing Early Christian Suffering* [Leiden: Brill, 2012]).

In this regard, the relevance of Paul's comment in Gal. 3:1 has long been neglected. There Paul mentions that he had "publicly exhibited" or "vividly displayed" Jesus Christ crucified "before your eyes," as if his preaching involved the reconstruction of Christ crucified in vivid display. One leading historian has this to say about that claim:

> It was characteristic of Paul's preaching that he focused on the fact that Jesus had died by crucifixion. He had made his hearers believe that they were present at the cross. No mere rhetorical tricks could achieve such an effect. Paul had to have the imagination to re-create the event for himself, and relive the appropriate emotions, before he could achieve the verbal vividness that he claims in Galatians 3:1. Paul's compulsion to replicate the crucifixion [in his public preaching] is explicable only if it made a huge impact on him.[38]

As Pauline scholars are increasingly coming to recognize, the force of Gal. 3:1 should not be underemphasized: Paul vividly described and/ or dramatically enacted the crucifixion of Jesus when he presented his gospel, capturing the imagination of his audience by depicting the crucifixion of Jesus in graphic detail within the pre-Constantinian world.[39] (He must, at the very least, have held out his arms to dramatize a crucified body for his audience.) If it is true that "crucifixion as a criminal by official authority was hardly the sort of teaching to find an immediately favorable response,"[40] it is also true that Paul's theologizing went directly and unapologetically against the grain of expectation on this matter. As Martin Hengel and Anna Maria Schwemer note, Gal. 3:1 suggests that Paul spoke of the crucifixion of Jesus using "a vivid narrative" so that his hearers were

---

38. Jerome Murphy-O'Connor, *Paul: His Story* (Oxford: Oxford University Press, 2006), 34.
39. See B. S. Davis, "The Meaning of *Proegraphē* in the Context of Galatians 3:1," *New Testament Studies* 45 (1999): 194–212; Steven Muir, "Vivid Imagery in Galatians 3:1—Roman Rhetoric, Street Announcing, Graffiti, and Crucifixions," *Biblical Theology Bulletin* 44 (2014): 76–86, especially 79–81.
40. Everett Ferguson, *Backgrounds of Early Christianity*, 3rd ed. (Grand Rapids: Eerdmans, 2003), 609.

"able to envisage this unspeakably offensive fact in a very concrete way."[41]

And if the impact of the crucifixion of Jesus was huge on Paul, that same apostle seems to have been intent on ensuring that his audiences were similarly impressed. He wanted them to know that their corporate meal involved the celebration of the "Lord's Supper" in which they "proclaim[ed] the Lord's death" (1 Cor. 11:26). That embodied proclamation of the Lord's crucified death probably was open to view by passersby within the house—precisely the situation described by Paul when he speaks of "outsiders or unbelievers" coming in among Jesus-devotees, almost randomly so (14:22–24, as noted above).

So too, in his letter to Philippian Christians, Paul instructed his readers to adopt an approach to life that replicates the life of Jesus Christ, who "humbled himself and became obedient to the point of death—even death on a cross" (Phil. 2:8). Here, astoundingly, crucifixion on a cross is a model around which Paul's audiences are to construct the whole of their life. There is no attempt to hide Jesus's crucifixion from view; instead, a symbol open to a shameful interpretation (by reference groups inclined to adopt such a view) has become a focal symbol that constructs a radically new worldview. Little wonder, then, that Paul refers to Jesus-followers as those who have been "crucified with Christ" (Rom. 6:6). Paul does not shy away from incorporating this metaphor even when writing to Christians in Rome who were, in a sense, directly under the nose of the emperor.

41. Martin Hengel and Anna Maria Schwemer, *Paul between Damascus and Antioch* (London: SCM Press, 1997), 17. Aliou Cissé Niang ("Seeing and Hearing Jesus Christ Crucified in Galatians 3:1 under Watchful Imperial Eyes," in *Text, Image, and Christians in the Graeco-Roman World*, ed. Aliou Cissé Niang and Carolyn Osiek [Eugene, OR: Pickwick, 2012], 175) speaks of Gal. 3:1 as illustrating how Jesus's death could have been interpreted as a "gory publicly displayed *votive offering* . . . whose redemptive work they [the Galatians] initially received." This possibility allows the crucifixion of Jesus to have had significance of a kind that remains underexplored within scholarship.

Neither did he pull back from describing those who die with the crucified Christ as coming alive with him with the power of a "newness of life" (Rom. 6:4). Paul especially claims the same to be true for himself. In a dramatic turn of phrase, Paul claims: "I have been crucified with Christ; and it is no longer I who live, but it is Christ who lives in me" (Gal. 2:19–20).

Paul, then, consistently placed the cross of Jesus front and center. What was shameful to him were a host of other things that crept into Christian communities (e.g., treating the body of Christ as a resource for personal advancement, failing to recognize the moral dimension of Christian identity, etc.), but not the cross itself. Perhaps, then, we should heed the words of Wayne Meeks when he notes that "Paul's most profound bequest to subsequent Christian discourse was his transformation of the reported crucifixion and resurrection of Jesus Christ into a multipurpose metaphor with vast generative and transformative power."[42]

Paul is only one example of the kind of thing that was being done throughout various sectors of the early Jesus-movement.[43] An essential project that many early Jesus-followers engaged in was not the covering up of the cross but the transformation of the cross as a primary theological symbol in order to capture the attention of their contemporaries. Accordingly, one of the most remarkable things about the early Christian movement is "that the early Christians did not dodge this reality [that is, the crucifixion of Jesus]. Instead, they found ways to embrace it."[44]

---

42. Wayne A. Meeks, *The Origins of Christian Morality: The First Two Centuries* (New Haven, CT: Yale University Press, 1995), 196.

43. For instance, the first-century Epistle to the Hebrews does this in a brief sound bite, describing Jesus as "the pioneer and perfecter of our faith, who for the sake of the joy that was set before him endured the cross, disregarding its shame, and [taking] his seat at the right hand of the throne of God" (Heb. 12:2).

44. Greg Carey, *Sinners: Jesus and His Earliest Followers* (Waco, TX: Baylor University Press, 2009), 113. As Horrell notes ("The Label Χριστιανός," 380): "This reversal of societal judgments

One of the ways they embraced the cross of Jesus was by weaving it intricately within a larger framework in a fashion that was unprecedented in the ancient world—that is, the cross of Jesus was interwoven with his resurrection.[45] The act of embedding Jesus's crucifixion in narrative garb that legitimated this "humiliating" tragedy was not something that happened relatively late in the development of Christianity but was one of the first things that some within the early Jesus-movement set out to accomplish.[46] Central to their mission was the transmutation of the cross's symbolic valence within the story of Jesus and the proclamation of that transmitted symbol within a narrative of triumph for the benefit of those with whom Jesus-followers came into contact (cf. Matt. 28:19–20). The transmutation of the cross from being an object of disgrace into a symbol of honor and glory (by way of its association with the resurrection) lies at the heart of virtually every text of the New Testament.[47]

This inseparable combination of elements created an unparalleled, stand-alone package that placed the crucifixion of Jesus within a matrix of power. This made the Christian message of the cross wholly distinctive—a *sui generis* phenomenon within the Greco-Roman world that had no analogy with ordinary conceptualizations of crucifixion. To think that the message about the cross of Jesus was inevitably constrained by normal parameters of perception is to

[concerning the cross] . . . was one means, essential to early Christianity, whereby attempts were made to construct and sustain a positive sense of group identity."

45. What Marcus J. Borg and John Dominic Crossan say of Paul is applicable to most forms of early Christianity (*The First Paul: Reclaiming the Radical Vision behind the Church's Conservative Icon* [London: SPCK, 2009], 123): "The cross and resurrection go together in Paul's thought and message. Resurrection gave meaning to the cross and the cross gave meaning to resurrection. Exploring the meanings of one necessarily involves the other."

46. See, for instance, Chris Keith and Tom Thatcher, "The Scar of the Cross: The Violence Ratio and the Earliest Christian Memories of Jesus," in *Jesus, the Voice, and the Text: Beyond The Oral and the Written Gospel*, ed. Tom Thatcher (Waco, TX: Baylor University Press, 2008), 197–214.

47. See, for instance, Hays, *Moral Vision of the New Testament*.

stumble at the first hurdle of historical inquiry. In the "good news" of the early Jesus-movement, the cross was embedded within a narrative of power and triumph—primary commodities in the ideological currency of the Greco-Roman world. It did not take Constantine to figure this out; it was already in the front of the shop window showcased by the earliest Christians. And along with power comes protection, something that was a rare commodity in the Greco-Roman world. If the cross was enmeshed within a narrative of protection from evil, some might well have seen its deficits to be far outweighed by its role in delivering Jesus-followers from evil and from death. In this light, it might actually be surprising if the cross never turned up as a Christian symbol in the three centuries prior to Constantine.

Relatedly, there was precedent within Greco-Roman mythology and historiography for the notion that suffering experienced by a hero or a deity could be beneficial for others. This is evidenced in Plutarch's depiction of Isis as a deity whose own "struggles" enabled her to be seen as empathetic toward those who faced their own hardships in life (*Isis and Osiris* 27):

> [Isis] was not indifferent to the contexts and struggles which she had endured, nor to her own wanderings nor to her manifold deeds of wisdom and many feats of bravery, nor would she accept oblivion and silence for them, but she intermingled in the most holy rites portrayals and suggestions and representations of her experiences at that time, and sanctified them, both as a lesson in godliness and an encouragement for men and women who find themselves in the clutch of like calamities.

David Balch has demonstrated that scenes of tragedy and suffering among the heroes and deities of Greco-Roman mythology are frequently depicted on the walls of houses, public buildings, and temples in ancient Rome, Pompeii, and Herculaneum.[48] This might suggest that those moments were deemed to be the turning points

45

in mythological narratives, with benefits flowing to others as a consequence of those moments of suffering.

The relationship between hardships endured and benefits for others takes on an almost "soteriological" tone in Lucan's account of the Roman civil war between Julius Caesar and Pompey, written in the early to mid-60s under Nero's reign. In one episode, Lucan records the speech of Cato with these words (*Bellum Civile* 2.306–319):

> Would it were possible for me, condemned by the powers of heaven and hell, to be the scapegoat for the nation! As hordes of foemen bore down Decius when he had offered his life, so may both armies pierce this body, may the savages from the Rhine aim their weapons at me; may I be transfixed by every spear, and may I stand between and intercept every blow dealt in this way! Let my blood redeem the nations, and my death pay the whole penalty incurred by the corruption of Rome. . . . Aim your swords at me alone, at me who fights a losing battle for despised law and justice. My blood, mine only, will bring peace to the people of Italy and end their suffering; the would-be tyrant need wage no war once I am gone.

These and other examples from the literary and material records demonstrate that the Greco-Roman world was not deficient in the grammar of suffering as a means whereby benefit flows to others. Evidently, the program of the early Christians of turning the cross of Jesus's suffering into a central pillar of "good news" seems quite at home within its Greco-Roman context.

If this phenomenon of transmuting the value of crucifixion within a narrative of power and triumph is evident already in the earliest years of the Jesus-movement, are we really to believe that, prior to Constantine, only the earliest Jesus-followers were adept at that skill?

---

48. David L. Balch, "The Suffering of Isis/Io and Paul's Portrait of Christ Crucified (Gal. 3:1): Frescoes in Pompeian and Roman Houses and in the Temple of Isis in Pompeii," *The Journal of Religion* 83 (2003): 24–55; and idem, "Paul's Portrait of Christ Crucified (Gal. 3:1) in Light of Paintings and Sculptures of Suffering and Death in Pompeian and Roman Houses," in *Early Christian Families in Context*, 84–108.

Were they exceptional in the program of inverting the symbolic value of the cross? Did this skill simply die off as the first generation of Jesus-followers gave way to successive pre-Constantinian generations? The evidence from later centuries suggests precisely the opposite, as we will see from both the material and the literary records of the pre-Constantinian centuries of the Common Era.[49]

Initial Implications

Old dogmas about the cross having been "bitterly humiliating" to Christians, for whom it would take "years before this deep rooted feeling could be overcome," are not necessarily compelling. As we have seen, Erich Dinkler long ago pronounced it "absolute dogma" in archaeological research that "the symbol of the cross makes its first appearance in the age of Constantine" (a claim he would later adjust somewhat).[50] These days, however, to impose a pre-Constantinian versus a post-Constantinian dividing line on any matter is quite

---

49. Another example of transforming the value of crucifixion might be evident in the *Oneirocritica*, Artemidorus's second-century ce book about interpreting dreams. One paragraph in book 2 deals with dreams about crucifixion (2.53): "It is opportune for a poor person [to dream of crucifixion]. For a crucified person is raised high, and nourishes many [sc. birds]. But it [a dream of crucifixion] means exposure of secrets. For a crucified person is readily visible. On the other hand, it signifies harm for rich people, since the crucified are stripped naked and lose their flesh. . . . It means freedom for slaves, since the crucified are no longer subject to any person. . . . To dream that one has been crucified in a city signifies that one will exercise rule over the place where the cross has been set up." Later (4.49), we hear: "Crucifixion dreams signify honor and wealth—honor, because the crucified person is in a very high position, and wealth, because he provides food for many birds of prey. In Greece, Menander dreamt that he was crucified in front of a temple of Zeus, Guardian of the City. He was appointed priest of this same god and became more well-known and wealthy as a result." Might crucifixion have been seen as a means of personal advancement—at least for those whose imaginations were immersed in crucifixion imagery to the extent that they went on even to dream about crucifixion? Is this relevant to an analysis of the rise of early Christianity in its Greco-Roman context? Some have recently suggested as much. See Justin J. Meggitt, "Laughing and Dreaming at the Foot of the Cross: Context and Reception of a Religious Symbol," in *Modern Spiritualities: An Inquiry*, ed. Laurence Brown, Bernard C. Farr, and R. Joseph Hoffmann (Oxford: Prometheus Books, 1997), 9–14; idem, "Artemidorus and the Johannine Crucifixion," *Journal of Higher Criticism* 5 (1998): 203–8; Joel Marcus, "Crucifixion as Parodic Exaltation," *Journal of Biblical Literature* 125 (2006): 73–87; Kelly Iverson, "The Centurion's Confession: A Performance-Critical Analysis of Mark 15:39," *Journal of Biblical Literature* 130 (2011): 329–50.

simply to operate with (1) an outmoded view of the first three centuries of emerging forms of Christianity and (2) an outmoded view of Christian postures toward the non-Christian world, and vice versa. Although Constantine represents a watershed of sorts, there may well have been "seepage" between the two sides of the watershed. When historical inquiry is released from the shackles of these old orthodoxies and old dogmas, new possibilities emerge, and nonstandard scenarios can and should be considered. This is all the more evident in light of the material record which, despite dogmatic voices to the contrary, cannot be ignored.

---

50. Erich Dinkler, "Comments on the History of the Symbol of the Cross," *Journal for Theology and the Church* 1 (1965): 132, the article first having been published in German in 1951, the quotation here being from page 157 of the 1951 article.

3

The Cross in a Jewish Cradle

The first stop on a tour of the pre-Constantinian material record must be Jerusalem. It is there that we first see crosses used in a fashion that will become instructive for interpreting texts and artifacts arising from later Christian contexts.

A hive of Jewish ossuaries (i.e., bone boxes) have been discovered in the vicinity of Jerusalem. These stone receptacles were intended to house the bones of the deceased a year after their death, once the flesh had fully decomposed. Generally speaking, these ossuaries date from about the middle of the second century BCE to the time of the first Jewish revolt in 66–70 CE.[1]

------

1. See Rachael Hachlili, "Ancient Jewish Burial," in *The Anchor Bible Dictionary*, ed. David Noel Freedman (New York: Doubleday, 1992), 1:789–94; David W. Chapman, *Ancient Jewish and Christian Perceptions of Crucifixion* (Grand Rapids: Baker Academic, 2008), 178–82; Lee Martin MacDonald, "The Burial of Jesus, Jewish Burial Practices, and Roman Crucifixion," in *The Tomb of Jesus and His Family? Exploring Ancient Jewish Tombs near Jerusalem's Walls*, ed. James H. Charlesworth (Grand Rapids: Eerdmans, 2013), 451. See, however, Craig A. Evans's helpful caution against drawing too sharp a boundary around these dates (*Jesus and the Ossuaries: What Jewish Burial Practices Reveal about the Beginning of Christianity* [Waco, TX: Baylor University Press, 2003], 28–29).

Some of these ossuaries bear the mark of an equilateral cross. Attempts to interpret these crosses as marks identifying the deceased as followers of Jesus have been unsuccessful. Some cross marks seem not to have functioned as symbols but, perhaps, simply as guides for placing the ossuary lid in its correct orientation.

Other kinds of intersecting marks appear occasionally on Jewish ossuaries, however. Two first-century Jewish ossuaries with distinctive shapes on their panels have drawn particular attention—the "Jehosah" ossuary, and ossuary 6 from the Talpiot Patio Tomb. Each of these ossuaries displays lines intersecting at ninety-degree angles within a solid rectangle. A case has been made for seeing the Talpiot ossuary as displaying a Christian cross. That case, however, is flawed.[2] Instead, as seems to be the case with the Jehosah ossuary, these intersecting lines are probably representations of the entrance into the holy of holies in the Jerusalem temple—the place where the presence of Israel's covenant deity was most concentrated within the sphere of creation (see fig 3.1).[3] But whatever they are, the intersecting lines on these ossuaries are not crosses per se, and are certainly not Christian symbols.

2. The case made by James D. Tabor and Simcha Jacobovici, *The Jesus Discovery: The Resurrection Tomb That Reveals the Birth of Christianity* (New York: Simon and Schuster, 2012), for seeing a Christian cross on this ossuary has been thoroughly debunked from several angles; see especially Christopher Rollston, "Review of *The Jesus Discovery: The New Archaeological Find That Reveals the Birth of Christianity*, by James D. Tabor and Simcha Jacobovici (New York: Simon and Schuster, 2012)," *Rollston Epigraphy: Ancient Inscriptions from the Levantine World*, April 12, 2012, http://www.rollstonepigraphy.com/?p=497.

3. This was proposed for the Jehosah ossuary by A. Grossberg, "Behold, The Temple: Is it Depicted on a Priestly Ossuary?" *Biblical Archaeology Review* 22, no. 3 (1996): 46–51, 66. The case has been made for ossuary 6 from the Talpiot tomb by Wim G. Meijer, "If It Walks Like a Duck: Ossuary 6 of the Talpiot 'Patio' Tomb Depicts Commonly Used Jewish Symbols," on *NT Blog*, Mark Goodacre, November 19, 2013, http://ntweblog.blogspot.com/2013/11/if-it-walks-like-duck-ossuary-6-of.html.

Figure 3.1. A reconstruction of the center inscription of the "Jehosah" ossuary.

A few other Jewish ossuaries, however, exhibit cross marks that are of particular importance. Several display two intersecting lines for purposes that are more than functional (in contrast to the lid markings) and that seem to serve a symbolic function (unlike the artistic depictions of the entrance into the holy of holies). These simple cross marks, whether in erect (+) or reclining (x) position, were prominently incised or drawn in charcoal in the middle of an ossuary panel or directly under the name of the person whose bones were inside (see figs. 3.2 through 3.5).[4] One further ossuary has a charcoal cross drawn on each of its four sides.[5]

Figure 3.2. A transcription of an inscription with the name "Yehudah" written above an equilateral cross.[6]

4. Erich Dinkler, "Comments on the History of the Symbol of the Cross," *Journal for Theology and the Church* 1 (1965): 136, 144.
5. See Jonathan J. Price, "Ossuary of Iesous Aloth with Greek Inscription, 1 c. CE," in *Corpus Inscriptionum Iudaeae/Palaestinae, Volume 1.2: Jerusalem, Part 2: 705-1120*, ed. Hannah M. Cotton et al. (Berlin: de Gruyter, 2012), 501–2. A cross also appears on an ossuary that had been taken from its original setting and moved into an ossuary warehouse in Jerusalem (Jack Finegan, *The Archaeology of the New Testament: The Life of Jesus and the Beginning of the Early Church* [Princeton, NJ: Princeton University Press, 1992], 361; see also Jack T. Sanders, *Schismatics, Sectarians, Dissidents, Deviants: The First One Hundred Years of Jewish-Christian Relations* [London: SCM Press, 1993], 35). The front of this ossuary includes the Greek letters eta and delta, over which stands an elaborately carved cross. It is possible that this cross was inscribed during the Byzantine period, when the Jewish ossuary may have been reused by a Christian. Accordingly, this ossuary cross is not included in this inventory.
6. From Finegan, *Archaeology of the New Testament*, 360.

Figure 3:3. A charcoal cross centrally located on the long side of a Jewish ossuary with three other crosses on each of the other sides of the ossuary.[7]

Figure 3:4. A deeply inscribed reclining equilateral cross (highlighted by a circle, added to the photo) under the popular female name "Shalamsion" on a Jewish ossuary near Jerusalem.[8]

7. Ibid., 366; see further E. L. Sukenik, "The Earliest Records of Christianity," *American Journal of Archaeology* 51 (1947): 351–65, plate 81.

Figure 3.5. The Nicanor ossuary, with a reclining equilateral cross centrally located on the side of the ossuary.[9]

These marks, then, were evidently deemed to be important. What might they have signified? They are unlikely to be mason's marks for orienting the inscriptions, since not all of the ossuaries on which they appear have inscriptions and, moreover, usually the inscriptions have little bearing in relation to the marks.[10] They are also unlikely to

---

8. From Finegan, *Archaeology of the New Testament*, 371.

9. Ibid., 358.

10. A common view is articulated by Eric M. Meyers and Mark A. Chauncey (*Alexander to Constantine: Archaeology of the Land of the Bible, Volume III.3* [New Haven, CT: Yale University Press, 2012], 186): these markings are "mason's marks meant to indicate how to align the lid or where to place a decoration or inscription." This interpretation is poorly suited to explain the ossuaries noted here.

be "merely crude decorations, in the absence of the more expensive incised ornamentation characteristic of ossuaries."[11]

As Erich Dinkler has shown, the most compelling explanation of prominently displayed ossuary crosses is that they are symbols rooted in Ezek. 9:4–6. In that passage, Israel's deity declares the following to his angelic servants:

> Go through the city, through Jerusalem, and put a mark on the foreheads of those who sigh and groan over all the abominations that are committed in it. . . . Pass through the city after him, and kill; your eye shall not spare, and you shall show no pity. Cut down old men, young men and young women, little children and women, but touch no one who has the mark. And begin at my sanctuary.

For our purposes, the key word here is "mark"—in Hebrew תו, or tav. Since tav is also the name of the final character in the Hebrew and Aramaic alphabet, the word "mark" was at times written as a symbol instead of being spelled out, that symbol being simply the final letter in the Hebrew alphabet. In the ancient Hebrew script, that letter could be represented by one of two formations: either (1) the standing cross, +, or (2) the reclining cross, x, in which the standing cross is rolled onto its side.[12] In this way, an equilateral cross mark

---

11. As suggested by Price, "Ossuary of Iesous Aloth with Greek Inscription, 1 c. CE," 502. Price shows no awareness of the possibility that these marks derive from Ezek. 9:4–6, as suggested here. As a consequence, he restricts the possible options for interpreting them to three: they were either (1) mason's marks, (2) crude decorations, or (3) marks of Christianity. The third option is ruled out on the basis that the cross "came into use long after these ossuaries were deposited in the cave" (502). Price is right that they are not Christian marks, but his lack of cognizance of the possibility that Ezekiel 9 provides the theological background for these marks is a surprising weakness in his engagement with these artifacts. The same deficiency is evident in Jonathan J. Price and Hannah M. Cotton, "Ossuary of Yehuda with Hebrew/Aramaic Inscription, 1 c. CE," in *Corpus Inscriptionum Iudaeae/Palaestinae, Volume 1.2: Jerusalem, Part 2: 705-1120*, who identify the mark on the Yehuda ossuary as "clearly a directional mason's mark," which looks more like a case of special pleading than reliable argumentation.

12. On the cross as a character in Semitic alphabets, see esp. Finegan, *Archaeology of the New Testament*, 339–42; Wilhelm Gesenius, *Gesenius' Hebrew Grammar*, trans. A. E. Cowley, ed. E. Kautzsch (Oxford: Clarendon, 1910), pullout table.

would serve as the mark of protection to be placed on the foreheads of those preserved from the wrath of Israel's deity.

Although this mark was presented in Ezekiel as being worn on foreheads, it had morphed to become a transferable mark of protection. According to Dinkler, the cross mark encapsulated "a total context of faith . . . in one sign"—a claim that today might be articulated in terms of an overarching narrative of salvation that is packaged up within the single symbol.[13] For this reason, the cross mark made its way onto the side of ossuaries of those who died in faithfulness to their covenant deity. As Dinkler notes, the mark on these Jerusalem ossuaries are best seen as "the *protective sign* for salvation at the coming day of judgment," indicating that "the person marked with the sign of Yahweh is Yahweh's property and therefore stands under his protection."[14]

Jewish texts from the first and second century BCE confirm that Ezekiel 9 fostered an interest in eschatological protective marks among some Jewish constituencies. So the *Psalms of Solomon* (from the first century BCE) speaks of the sign or mark of God being "upon the righteous that they may be saved" (15:6). Similarly, in the *Damascus Document* from the Qumran community near the Dead Sea (middle of the second century BCE) we read the following in 19:9–13:

> But those who give heed to God are "the poor of the flock" [Zech. 11:7]: they will escape in the time of punishment, but all the rest will be handed over to the sword when the Messiah of Aaron and of Israel comes, just as it happened during the time of the first punishment, as Ezekiel said, "Make a mark on the foreheads of those who moan and lament" [Ezek. 9:4], but the rest were given to the sword that makes retaliation for covenant violations.

13. Dinkler, "Comments on the History of the Symbol of the Cross," 145.
14. Ibid., 138. Emphasis original.

Since the *Psalms of Solomon* breathes the air of mainstream (probably Pharisaic) Judaism and the *Damascus Document* serves as a defining document for the sectarian Judaism of the Dead Sea community, it is notable that this interest in protective signs, indebted to an interpretation of Ezek. 9:4–6, is evident in two streams of Second Temple Judaism. Of course, neither of these Jewish texts reveals how the "mark" was to be formed. But since the word "mark" (תו or tav) could be written as an equilateral cross, that shape is the most obvious candidate. And since neither text reveals to its readers what the shape of the "mark" actually was (even though the mark was crucial in serving as a form of eschatological protection), it must have been assumed that readers of these documents, whether they were in mainstream or sectarian sectors of Judaism, knew the shape of the mark. The *Psalms of Solomon* and the *Damascus Document* indicate that a symbol of eschatological protection had already been circulating in pre-Christian forms of Judaism, and that mark was most likely an equilateral cross.

This is probably why the Greek Septuagint refers to this "mark" in an articular construction in both Ezek. 9:4 and 9:6 (lxx: τὸ σημεῖον), whereas four other occurrences of the word in Ezekiel have no article preceding them (4:3; 20:12, 20; 39:15). (Precisely the same distinction is maintained in the Vulgate, which generally employs the word *signum* [Ezek. 4:3; 20:12, 20] except in 9:4 and 9:6, where it uses the word *thau*.) This suggests that the "mark" of Ezekiel 9 was a "monadic" or "well-known" mark that was "familiar to readers" in identifying a "one-of-a-kind noun"—a mark par excellence that was "in a class by itself."[15]

---

15. Here I borrow the terms Daniel B. Wallace uses to define the "monadic," "well-known," and "*par excellence*" articular infinitives (*Greek Grammar beyond the Basics: An Exegetical Syntax of the New Testament* [Grand Rapids: Zondervan, 1996], 732).

In light of this convergence of evidence from both the material and the literary records, Dinkler's interpretation of particular Jewish ossuaries from first-century Jerusalem has strong explanatory force. The "mark" of two intersecting lines at right angles to each other, which figures prominently on several Jerusalem ossuaries, had already been incorporated within Jewish symbolism prior to the early Jesus-movement. Rooted in the imagery of Ezekiel 9, that mark was bestowed with eschatological import as a sign of identification and a means of protection.[16]

We would be remiss, then, if we failed to ask whether this background might have fostered interest in the same symbol within earliest Christianity, not least since the Jesus-movement emerged from the cradle of Judaism, from which it drew many of its primary theological resources.[17] In fact, as we will see, Ezek. 9:4–6 proved to be of interest to Christian theologians throughout the first three centuries of the Common Era, where the "mark" of Ezekiel 9 was interpreted as the cross of Jesus. This was true of the author of 5 Ezra in the first half of the second century, of Tertullian in the early third century, and of Cyprian in the middle of the third century, as demonstrated in chapter 7 below. It was arguably also the case for the author of the Johannine Apocalypse at the end of the first century and

---

16. For this reason, Byron R. McCane's claim that "no sources from the early Roman period associate the ossuary with belief in the resurrection" (*Roll Back the Stone: Death and Burial in the World of Jesus* [Harrisburg, PA: Trinity Press International, 2003], 43) seems to miss the mark. I see no reason to dispute his case that the ossuaries testify to a form of Hellenistic individualization within Judean Judaism (46–47), but this is not in conflict with the eschatological "mark" of Ezekiel 9 that appears on several of the Jerusalem ossuaries.

17. I remain dubious, however, about the marks found in the margins of some scrolls from the Qumran community, such as the Isaiah scroll. The claim that these are highlighters to mark passages about the messiah (see Finegan, *Archaeology of the New Testament*, 346–48) is unconvincing, for a number of reasons. Note, for instance, that similar marks are found in non-Jewish texts as well, with the *chi* (X) probably signaling passages that the reader found to be most "useful" (*chrēstos*, which of course begins with a *chi*); see especially William Johnson, "The Ancient Book," in *The Oxford Handbook of Papyrology*, ed. R. S. Bagnall (Oxford: Oxford University Press, 2009), 257–81.

for the third-century author of the *Testament of Solomon*, as we will see in chapter 4 below.

For now, it is enough to hear the interpretation of Ezekiel 9 in the time of Origen, the Christian theologian from the mid-third century. He recounts an occasion on which he asked Jews what teachings they had passed on regarding the significance of the Hebrew letter tav (the question itself being indicative of Origen's interest in the theological interpretation of the shape of the cross). Of the three answers he received, the third came from a Christian Jew ("one of those who believe in Christ") who said "the form of the *tav* in old [Hebrew] script resembles the cross (*tou staurou*), and it predicts the mark which is to be placed on the foreheads of the Christians" (*Selecta in Ezehielem* 9 [*Patrologia Graeca* 13: 800–801]).[18] This passage testifies to the continuing knowledge, as late as the middle of the third century, that the mark of Ezekiel 9 could be formed by the intersection of two lines—a cross, taken to be a prophetic "prediction" of what is to come.[19]

Of course, in its original Jewish context, this symbol of eschatological protection had nothing to do with crucifixion, and certainly not the crucifixion of the Messiah. It was only when the Christian imagination began to explore scriptural precedents that it found a ready-made symbol and took that symbol to another stage in its theological development—specifically, as representing the cross of Christ, as exemplified in the quotation from Origen. In this way, the Ezekiel passage was available for acquisition and open to further theological development by the Christian imagination.

18. Notice that the formation of the cross in this third-century text is imagined as equilateral or x, instead of Tertullian's conceptualization of it as T cross, as noted in chapter 7 below.
19. G. K. Beale (*The Book of Revelation: A Commentary on the Greek Text* [Grand Rapids: Eerdmans, 1999], 410) is right to note that Ezekiel 9 "facilitated a Jewish-Christian identification of the *taw* sign (+ or x) with the cross."

What we are witnessing, then, is the transference of a religious symbol from one sphere of religion to another—a phenomenon noted by Erwin Goodenough in his preeminent study *Jewish Symbols in the Greco-Roman Period*. He writes: "When a new movement wants a powerful symbol, it usually finds satisfaction in revising one of the primordial symbols rather than in inventing a new one, and we presume that this happens because an old symbol has an inherent symbolic power of some kind at least dormant in itself."[20]

It should not be surprising to find that the Jewish cradle in which Christianity initially lay provided resources utilized by the early Jesus-movement. One of those resources was the sign of two intersecting perpendicular lines—a sign that was thought to enhance eschatological protection by the deity of Israel. Did that ready-made theological symbol merge with Christian theologizing about the cross? As we will see, the data suggests that this natural coupling did, in fact, occur, and at a relatively early date in the emergence of Christian identity.

---

20. Erwin R. Goodenough, *Jewish Symbols in the Greco-Roman Period* (Princeton, NJ: Princeton University Press, 1953), 47.

4

The Cross in Textual Images

We have seen that two intersecting perpendicular lines seem to have played a role as a mark of theological significance in some sectors of first-century Judaism, and we know that the Constantinian era started the cross on a meteoric rise as the preeminent symbol of Christian devotion. We want now to probe the years in between, to determine whether, to what extent, and in what ways the cross was used as a Christian symbol.

Two early Christian texts from the late first and early second centuries are important in this regard, for three reasons—temporal, theological, and artistic.

1. Temporally, they indicate that Christian reflection on the shape of the cross was occurring at a relatively early date.
2. Theologically, they demonstrate that the cross had become an object of diverse theological reflection.
3. Artistically, they illustrate the diversity in which the shape of the cross was being conceptualized by some early Christians.

Establishing these contours at the outset will assist us when we turn to the material record in further chapters.

The *Epistle of Barnabas*

Pseudonymously attributed to the missionary partner of the apostle Paul, the *Epistle of Barnabas* is one of the earliest extant Christian texts. A number of scholars are content to date its composition to the mid-90s.[1] Most place it in the first half of the second century, having been written prior to 132 in the eastern Mediterranean region (probably Alexandria).[2]

In chapter 12 of the *Epistle of Barnabas*, a cruciform shape is linked to the success of the Hebrew people in battle. The sign of the cross, it is claimed, had long ago been revealed in Israel's history when the Hebrew people, assaulted by enemy forces, were delivered from attack (elaborating Exod. 17:9–14). It happened this way, says the author (12.2). The Spirit of God revealed to Moses "that he should make a figure of the cross [τύπον σταυροῦ] and of Him [i.e., Jesus] about to suffer thereon; for unless they put their trust in Him, they shall be overcome for ever." According to the *Epistle of Barnabas*, whenever Moses abandoned his own weapons and raised out his hands so that his body had formed the shape of a cross, Israel acquired the tactical advantage, and whenever he lowered his hands, Israel lost the advantage.[3] Here the author focuses his audience's attention on

---

1. The evidence for this comes from the *Epistle of Barnabas* 4.4–5 and especially 16.3–4. See John Dominic Crossan, *The Cross That Spoke: The Origins of the Passion Narrative* (San Francisco: HarperCollins, 1992), 121 (also idem, *The Historical Jesus: The Life of a Jewish Mediterranean Peasant* [San Francisco: HarperCollins, 1991], 431); and especially William Horbury, "Jewish-Christian Relations in Barnabas and Justin Martyr," in *Jews and Christians: The Parting of the Ways, a.d. 70-135*, ed. J. D. G. Dunn (Tübingen: Mohr Siebeck, 1992), 315–46.

2. Robert A. Kraft (*Barnabas and the Didache* [New York: Nelson, 1965], 55) claims that the *Epistle of Barnabas* is "the work of a Christian teacher whose thought, in general, is oriented towards Alexandria, and whose area of ministry is in northeast Egypt."

3. The passage speaks of Moses abandoning his own weapons in the process, piling them up on top of each other in order to raise his weaponless arms in the shape of a cross. The point is

the shape of the cross as the basis for this christological interpretation of Scripture.

The cross is also found in chapter 9 of the *Epistle of Barnabas*, when the author recounts a secret tradition about Abraham—the so-called mysteries of the three letters. To this tradition the author applies "isopsephic" decoding—a common practice in the ancient world, in which Greek letters were given numerical values according to an established formula and then interpreted in relation to those values. So, for instance, an inscription from the ancient city of Smyrna declares, "I love her whose number is 731." The three Greek letters used by the inscriber have the values of 700, 30, and 1 respectively, obviously adding up to 731. The woman's name was probably "Anthousa," the letters of that Greek name also equaling that number.[4]

Applying the same practice to a secret scriptural tradition that he calls the "mysteries of the three letters," the author of *Epistle of Barnabas* writes the following (9.8):

> Abraham, the first who enjoined circumcision, looking forward in spirit to Jesus, practiced that rite, having received the mysteries of the three letters. For [the scriptural tradition] says, "And Abraham circumcised ten, and eight, and three hundred men of his household." What, then, was the knowledge given to him in this? Learn the eighteen first, and then the three hundred. The ten and the eight are thus denoted—ten by *I* [the Greek letter iota having the value 10], and eight by *H* [the Greek letter eta having the value 8]. You have Jesus [i.e., the first two letters of the name "Jesus," IHΣOYΣ or *Iēsous*]. And because the cross was to express the grace [of our redemption] by the letter *T* [the Greek letter tau having the value 300], he says also, "Three Hundred." He signifies, therefore, Jesus by two letters, and the cross by one.

made, it seems, in order to avoid the impression that confidence came to Israel through Moses's weaponry, or that victory is ultimately rooted in the superiority of military tactics.

4. This is proposed by Roger Bagnall, *Everyday Writing in the Greco-Roman East* (Berkeley: University of California Press, 2011), 15.

The author claims that Jesus and the cross are both embedded within this Abrahamic tradition. Through the vehicle of theological isopsephy, the cross is functioning as a symbol that bears the weight of a christological reading of this secret tradition. And the shape of the cross is itself the basis for this theological isopsephy.[5]

More will be said about these passages from the *Epistle of Barnabas* later in this chapter. For now, one of the latest texts of the New Testament offers important resources for further consideration of the place of the cross in early Christian imagination—the Johannine Apocalypse, also known as Revelation.

The Book of Revelation

The Johannine Apocalypse began to be circulated in its final form among prominent Christian groups probably in the last decade of the first century (although some scholars place it earlier, in the 60s). That text propagates a highly symbolic narrative about the destruction of all power that opposes the will of the creator. In the process, it incorporates the following comment (7:2–3):

> I saw another angel ascending from the rising of the sun, having the seal of the living God, and he called with a loud voice to the four angels who had been given power to damage earth and sea, saying, "Do not damage the earth or the sea or the trees, until we have marked the servants of our God with a seal on their foreheads."

Of note here is the mention of "the seal" or signet ring (σφραγῖδα) "of the living God" (compare 2 Cor. 1:22), which is used by an angel to place marks of protection on the foreheads of Jesus-followers who are thereby protected from the impending cosmic disaster. The same is referred to later in the apocalyptic narrative, as disasters

---

5. The same theological isopsephy can be found later in Clement (*Stromata* 6.11.84.3), who is probably borrowing from the *Epistle of Barnabas*. The number 318 can be found in Gen. 14:14, but not in relation to the "mysteries of the three letters" recounted in the *Epistle of Barnabas*.

come on "only those people who do not have the seal of God [τὴν σφραγῖδα τοῦ θεοῦ] on their foreheads" (9:4)—in contrast to the mark of the beast that is said to be emblazoned on the foreheads of others (13:16–17; 14:9–11; 16:2; 19:20; 20:4).

Various Jewish texts depict the deity of Israel having a seal, either as a way of protecting his people and his creation or as a means of controlling malevolent forces (Job 9:7; Sirach 17:22; *Testament of Moses* 12.9; *Apocalypse of Moses* 42.1; *Prayer of Manasseh* 3). Some magical papyri display interest in this divine seal or signet ring, calling on "the powerful name and seal of the great deity" (*PGM* VII.583; cf. *PGM* I.306 and III.226) and identifying that "great deity" who has a seal by means of names applicable to the deity of Israel (*PGM* III.266-67; IV.1485–86, 1534–35, 1561, 1621, 2315, 2326, 3053; VII.220, 311, 595–96).[6] Clearly, the ancient imagination was enamored by the notion that an almighty deity had a protective signet ring that was used to bestow a powerful mark of protection on his people.

Ideally, an ancient signet ring displayed on its bezel either something of keen interest to its owner or (if it was used as a stamp ring) the name or the identity of the owner in some fashion. So the ancient imagination would inevitably be acutely interested in what was engraved on that signet ring.

If we are disappointed by the fact that the text of Revelation does not articulate what the bezel of the divine signet ring displayed, the informed ancient imagination might not have been so disappointed. When Revelation mentions "the signet ring of the living God" that marks out "the servants of our God with a seal on their foreheads"

---

6. See esp. David E. Aune, *Revelation 6–16*, Word Biblical Commentary 52b (Nashville: Thomas Nelson, 1998), 453. And see further the evidence he cites on 453–54, including various Jewish texts and artifacts that build on the seal or signet ring of Israel's deity (along with the Christian text *Testament of Solomon* 1.6–7; 10.6; 15.7).

(7:2–3) and protects them from tumultuous dangers (9:4), it is building on the imagery of Ezek. 9:4–6. This is not controversial, being commonly accepted by scholars.[7] As we have already seen, however, the material and literary records testify to the fact that Ezekiel's "mark" of protection placed on the forehead was known to be the intersection of two perpendicular lines, as in the equilateral or x that represented the tav of the ancient Hebrew script. In chapter 3 above, we noted that this notion tracks all the way from pre-Christian Jewish texts and artifacts through to several Christian texts of the second and third centuries (see further examples in chapter 7 below). Right in the middle of that trajectory of tradition falls the Johannine Apocalypse. When we read, then, about a "signet ring of the living God" that places a seal on the foreheads of his people, and when we recognize that the imagery draws directly on that of Ezek. 9:4–6, we must suppose that an audience having a resourceful or informed mind in its midst could have come to the view that the mark placed on the foreheads of the people of "the living God" was the mark of the cross.[8]

According to Greg Beale, the mark of the divine Lord and the mark of the beast may "connote that the followers of Christ and the beast both are stamped with the image (i.e., character) of their respective leaders."[9] In this frame of reference, the signet ring of the sovereign Lord displays his character in relation to the cross. But there is more to this than the display of divine character. The mark

---

7. So, for instance, Richard Bauckham, *The Climax of Prophecy: Studies on the Book of Revelation* (Edinburgh: T & T Clark, 1993), 217: "The echo [within 7:2–3 and 9:4] of Ezekiel 9:4–6 . . . is clear." Compare G. K. Beale, *The Book of Revelation: A Commentary on the Greek Text* (Grand Rapids: Eerdmans, 1999), 409–10; M. Eugene Boring, *Revelation* (Louisville: Westminster John Knox, 1989), 128; Adela Yarbro Collins, *The Apocalypse* (Wilmington, DE: Michael Glazier, 1983), 52.

8. Compare Gerhard A. Krodel, *Revelation* (Minneapolis: Augsburg Fortress, 1989), 183: the identification mark of the signet ring would have been understood to be "in the form of a cross or an X [the first letter of the name of Christ]"; so too Robert H. Mounce, *The Book of Revelation* (Grand Rapids: Eerdmans, 1977), 157.

9. Beale, *Book of Revelation*, 716.

also plays out in relation to the divine "name" that is said to be placed on the foreheads of God's people (14:1 and 22:4).[10] Are both a mark and the divine name written on their foreheads? Apocalyptic imagery in general allows for images to be piled on top of each other, but in this case we are probably to imagine that one and the same thing is being imaged. As some have postulated, the "mark" of Ezekiel 9 was understood in Jewish circles "as representing the divine name."[11] This would make perfect sense in relation to the combining of images in the course of Revelation (7:2–3; 9:4; 14:1; 22:4), and in relation to the Jerusalem ossuaries considered in chapter 3. The cross mark that those ossuaries exhibit may have been regarded as the representation of the name of the deity to whom the deceased owed allegiance. Understood as a mark of possession and belonging, it was a graphic way of symbolizing that the contents of the ossuary belonged to Israel's covenant deity. "Property of Israel's God" might be one way of translating the mark's significance. Since the ossuaries had the name of Israel's deity on them, no other power could tamper with them.[12]

Everett Ferguson brings all this together in his interpretation of the mark left by the divine signet ring of Rev. 7:2–3: "Some tracing (perhaps with oil) of a mark representing the divine name (Ezek 9:4, probably the Hebrew letter *tav*) on the forehead . . . marked that person as belonging to the Lord."[13] The Johannine seer probably

---

10. Beyond Revelation, see 2 Tim. 2:19, where God's seal contains passages from Scripture, including one that references "the name of the Lord."

11. Beale, *Book of Revelation*, 410. So also John P. M. Sweet, *Revelation* (Philadelphia: Westminster, 1979), 148: "Ezekiel's mark (*tau*, the last letter of the Hebrew alphabet—written in the old script or x) was currently taken by Jews as the Divine Name."

12. This gives meaning to what the risen Lord says to the church at Philadelphia in Rev. 3:12: "I will write on him the name of my God . . . and my own new name." If the "mark" of Ezekiel 9, represented by the Paleo-Hebrew tav, was thought to represent the name of Israel's deity, it is easy to see how the same mark could be "co-opted" by the resurrected Jesus as his "new name"—a case of one symbol serving to combine traditional and novel meanings simultaneously.

assumed that his readers would recognize the point, either already being cognizant of the symbolic interpretation of Ezek. 9:4–6 or soon to be introduced to it through Christian pedagogy. Evidently, then, the interpretation of Ezekiel 9 that was displayed on Jerusalem ossuaries and took on new meaning in Christian texts of the second and third century was already in the toolbox of Christian instruction in the late first century, from which audiences of the Johannine Apocalypse could draw interpretative resources.

Here we can recall Richard Bauckham's view of the requirements for reading the Johannine Apocalypse. Bauckham demonstrates time and again that the text of Revelation is packed full of subtle, unarticulated intricacies that require the audience to operate as textual detectives if those intricacies are to be fully appreciated—detectives both of the apocalyptic text itself and its scriptural precursors. According to Bauckham, "Revelation was evidently designed to convey its message to some significant degree on first hearing (cf. 1:3), but also progressively to yield fuller meaning to closer acquaintance and assiduous study."[14]

Along similar lines, even if some audiences happened to be unaware of the theological significance of Ezek. 9:4–6, the author may well have imagined that the "fuller meaning" of the "signet ring of God" would become apparent to them in the course of an ongoing Christian pedagogy.

As we will see in chapter 7 below, one Christian author from before the mid-second century (the author of 5 Ezra) seems to have

---

13. Everett Ferguson, *Baptism in the Early Church: History, Theology, and Liturgy in the First Five Centuries* (Grand Rapids: Eerdmans, 2009), 196.

14. Bauckham, *Climax of Prophecy*, 1. Bauckham goes on to note that this level of textual artistry "would not have been easy to achieve. It is further evidence of the meticulous composition of the book. . . . We could say that he buried in the literary composition of his work theological significance which few readers have subsequently unearthed, though it may well be that, among his first readers, at least his fellow-prophets would know better than later readers what to look for" (33).

interpreted Rev. 7:2–3 in precisely this way, having recognized the "fuller meaning" waiting to be recognized within the text. For now, it is enough to note how the *Testament of Solomon* also interprets the mark of Revelation 7 as the sign of the cross. The *Testament of Solomon* is a Christian text of the third century that develops an earlier Jewish text that is no longer extant but that seems to have derived from the first or second century CE. In one episode (17.1–5), Solomon encounters a demonic spirit. When he requires the spirit to identify itself, it self-identifies as "a lecherous spirit of a giant man who died in a massacre in the age of giants." The spirit explains its strategy this way:

> My home is in inaccessible places. My activity is this: I seat myself near dead men in the tombs and at midnight I assume the form of the dead; if I seize anyone, I immediately kill him with the sword. If I should not be able to kill him, I cause him to be possessed by a demon and to gnaw his own flesh to pieces and the saliva of his jowls to flow down.

Next Solomon requires him to reveal the spiritual power by which the spirit can be thwarted. Referring to Jesus Christ, the spirit announces: "He who is about to return (as) Savior thwarts me. If his mark is written on (one's) forehead, it thwarts me, and because I am afraid of it, I quickly turn and flee from him. This is the sign of the cross." Here again we witness a tradition, ultimately rooted in Ezek. 9:4–6 and testified to on Jewish ossuaries and in early Christian texts, in which a mark is written on the forehead, consisting in the conjoining of two interlocking perpendicular lines. To the eyes of Christians, it was clear what those interlocking lines signified.

The Shape of the Cross

Although the *Epistle of Barnabas* and the Johannine Apocalypse do not provide us with material remains showing Christian crosses inscribed or artistically presented on ancient media, they nonetheless help us to reconstruct how the cross was being conceptualized at the end of the first century and the beginning of the second century. In fact, these three literary passages (*Epistle of Barnabas* 9 and 12, and Rev. 7:2–3) display different conceptualizations of the formation of the cross in each instance.

The *Epistle of Barnabas* 12 depicts Moses holding out his unweaponed hands by his sides after being commanded to make a figure that replicated both "the cross" and "Him about to suffer thereon." The image, then, is not of Moses replicating a T cross but, in fact, replicating a body cross, †. We will later take note of other early Christian texts that imagine the cross in the same formation.

Notice, however, that the cross is imagined in a different formation in the *Epistle of Barnabas* 9. Speaking of the cross having the value of the Greek letter tau, chapter 9 envisions the cross as a T, with the crossbeam at the top of the vertical post. This is a formation that the *Epistle of Barnabas* 9 shares with other early Christian texts and artifacts, as will be seen in other chapters below.

Accordingly, both the body cross and the T cross are present in the *Epistle of Barnabas*. With only two short chapters separating these two discussions of the cross, the author of the *Epistle of Barnabas* shifts from one conceptualization to the other, as if the two patterns could sit alongside each other without distraction, being used for different rhetorical purposes. Evidently this author found the cross to be chock-full of theological symbolism and sought to exploit the polyvalence of its shape in any way possible. Differences in the shape of the cross were not to be avoided, since each distinct shape fostered different possibilities for theological discourse.

Interestingly, however, the Johannine Apocalypse opens the possibility of a third formation for the cross, since, as we have seen, it is likely to foster the notion of the cross in equilateral formation.

All this is to say that in two Christian texts that straddle the end of the first century (i.e., the Johannine Apocalypse and *Epistle of Barnabas*), two theologians engage three scriptural passages (one allegedly a tradition) to draw out three different christological applications, making use of three different cruciform configurations in the process.[15]

Besides the diversity of formations evident in these two Christian texts, it is intriguing that so much theological import is being given to the cross. Note especially the implications of Rev. 7:2–3. In the ancient world, signet rings usually conveyed either the leading characteristics of a person's identity or an image that was attractive to the ring's owner. If a cross is thought to be engraved on the signet ring of the almighty deity, that symbol lies at the heart of the identity and/or affections of that deity. By implication, it is also pertinent to the followers of that deity, and the Johannine Apocalypse explains why that should be the case—that is, that symbol offers them protection.

The question arises: When the Johannine Apocalypse circulated among Jesus-followers of the second and third centuries, did its readers see similar attraction in the cross as a theological symbol? Material and textual indicators suggest that they did. In fact, each of the three early formations of the cross that we have seen in this chapter reappear in the material and textual record of Christians in the second and third centuries, as we will see in the following chapter.

---

15. Richard Viladesau explains it in brief in this fashion (*The Beauty of the Cross: The Passion of Christ in Theology and the Arts, from the Catacombs to the Eve of the Renaissance* [Oxford: Oxford University Press, 2006], 42): "In the vision of the prophet Ezekiel (Ez. 9:4–6), those who are being saved from the wrath of God are marked with a cross (i.e., the letter *tav*) on their foreheads. There is some evidence that eschatologically oriented Jewish groups, inspired by this text, had taken up the practice of signing of themselves with the *tav*/cross by the time of Jesus. The early Christians connected the passage from Ezekiel with the cross of Christ."

5

The Cross in the Material Record

It is one thing to recognize how the cross was being formed in the mental imaging of two early Christian authors. It is another thing to find those mental images transferred to ancient artistic media. This chapter surveys most of the material evidence testifying to the cross as a devotional symbol among pre-Constantinian Christians. It will demonstrate that, even in the pre-Constantinian era, the cross was employed by Christians as a visual, artistic symbol of their faith. The cross was not simply formed in conceptual images enjoyed by the mind. Instead, at times it became concretized as a visual symbol, an image embedded within artistic media.

Rome and Its Port City

The cross is depicted in various third-century inscriptions from the city of Rome and its environs in the pre-Constantinian period. One of these inscriptions is commonly referenced in discussions of early Christianity. Found on the Palatine Hill near the imperial residence in Rome, it portrays a person by the name Alexamenos in the process of worshiping his deity, and dates perhaps to the early third century.[1] The deity depicted is not one of the traditional Roman deities but one hanging on a cross, a cross in the shape of a T. The tone of this inscription is one of mockery, as seen by the fact that the inscriber has depicted the crucified deity as having the head of a donkey (see fig. 5.1)—referencing the view that Christians worshiped a donkey-headed deity (see Minucius Felix, *Octavius* 9.3; 28.7; Tertullian, *Apology* 16.12). One interpreter imagines this inscription, which features the words "Alexamenos worships his deity" or "Alexamenos, worship [your] deity," to have been "drawn by a palace page with cruel schoolboy humor to mock the faith of a fellow slave."[2]

Does this artifact have any significance regarding Christian use of the cross? The common view is that it does not. Instead, it merely shows that non-Christians knew enough about Christian beliefs to mock the notion of a crucified deity. But even if this is all that the Alexamenos inscription reveals, that much is at least suggestive; if Christians were trying to hide the crucifixion of Jesus from their contemporaries, they were not doing a very good job of it.

1. On the early-third-century date of the Alexamenos inscription, see I. Di Stafano Manzella, *Le iscrizioni dei cristiani in Vaticano: Materiali e contributi scientifici per una mostra epigrafica* (Vatican City: Edizioni Quasar, 1997), 192–94; Felicity Harley and Jeffrey Spier, "Magical Amulet with the Crucifixion," in *Picturing the Bible: The Earliest Christian Art*, ed. Jeffrey Spier (New Haven, CT: Yale University Press, 2007), 227–28.

2. Richard Viladesau, *The Beauty of the Cross: The Passion of Christ in Theology and the Arts, from the Catacombs to the Eve of the Renaissance* (Oxford: Oxford University Press, 2006), 19. He also notes that the inscription "reflects the Roman belief that the Jews worshiped a god with the head of an ass—a notion that was apparently also carried over to Christians" (20).

Figure 5.1. A reconstruction of the Alexamenos inscription.

But does the Alexamenos inscription do more? Does it suggest that the cross was recognized as a Christian symbol prior to Constantine? Some, such as Felicity Harley-McGowan, think that it does. In her study of early Christian depictions of crucifixion, Harley-McGowan writes:

> This visual conception of a crucifixion . . . suggests a "pagan," or non-Christian's awareness of two things: firstly, the significance of Jesus' Crucifixion (at least in terms of it being a powerful and efficacious symbol); and secondly, a consciousness of the existence of Christian representations of the crucifixion by the early 3rd century AD.[3]

---

3. Felicity Harley-McGowan, "The Constanza Carnelian and the Development of Crucifixion Iconography in Late Antiquity," in *"Gems of Heaven": Recent Research on Engraved Gemstones*

"Crucifixion," "powerful symbol," "representations," "early third century"—these terms are rarely placed together in positive relationship when discussing the cross prior to Constantine. But they represent one historian's challenge to a long-standing view about the absence of the cross in pre-Constantinian forms of Christianity.

The Alexamenos inscription notwithstanding, other evidence from the environs of Rome leads us toward the same conclusion. In 1919 an underground sepulcher was discovered on the Viale Manzoni in Rome, west of the Porta Maggiore. It contains several tomb chambers. A mosaic was found in one of the chambers, commemorating some individuals of free status from among the Aurelia household. They are said to be "brothers," although the list mentions not only men (i.e., Onesimus, Papirus, and Felicissimus) but also one woman (Prima, said to be a virgin). Within the chambers of the Aurelii sepulcher is a considerable amount of artwork, most of which has a religious dimension. One painting is of significance. It depicts a man whose right hand points directly to a body cross. According to William Tabbernee, this "is a clear indication of Christianity."[4] The sepulcher is dated to a time before 282 CE.

Just beyond Rome, in its closest port city, Ostia, a group of symbols were incised into one area of flooring in room 6 of the Baths of Neptune (region 2, insula 4; see fig. 5.2). The symbols etched by users of this public room appear in figure 5.3.

in *Late Antiquity c. AD 200–600*, ed. Chris Entwistle and Noël Adams (London: The British Museum Press, 2011), 218; she reiterates these opinions on 219. Here she closely echoes the words of Jeffrey Spier, *Late Antique and Early Christian Gems* (Wiesenbaden: Reichert, 2007), 75; see below at footnote 52.

4. William Tabbernee, *Montanist Inscriptions and Testimonia* (Washington, DC: Catholic University of America Press, 1996), 128–29. See his fuller discussion on pages 124–31.

Figure 5.2. Room 6 of the Ostian Baths of Neptune.

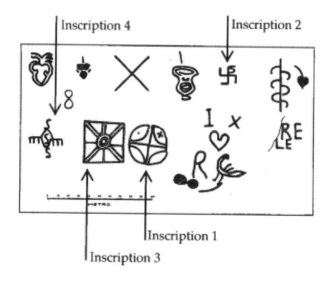

Figure 5.3. Christian symbols in room 6 of the Baths of Neptune in Ostia.[5]

5. From G. Becatti, *Scavi di Ostia, IV: Mosaici e Pavimenti Marmorei, Vols. I & II* (Rome: Libreria della Stato, 1961), figure 17. The symbols are not as they were found, but have been extracted from their positions and grouped together in this figure. Moreover, I have rotated inscription 2 ninety degrees counterclockwise, since I take it to include a staurogram—something that was

In his definitive study of Ostia Antica, Giovanni Becatti, an eminent archaeologist from the mid-twentieth century and onetime director of excavations at Ostia Antica, claims that these inscriptions are Christian symbols (an interpretation shared by Ostian scholar Jan Theo Bakker).[6] Whether that is true for all the inscriptional marks on this floor, it is nonetheless notable that (as I will demonstrate in the paragraphs below) at least four of these symbols incorporate the symbol of the cross, one of which incorporates the name Jesus while another incorporates a variant form of a Christian staurogram.

Note, for instance, how the shape of an equilateral cross serves as the scaffolding for one of the most interesting of all the cross formations among these symbols—inscription 4. Although inscription 4 looks like a series of artistic scribbles, it unpacks to spell out the Latin word *Iesus*, or "Jesus," twice—with the clever styler of this fascinating construction having laid the letters along the two axes of an equilateral cross. It is constructed in the following fashion, from left to right (compare also fig. 5.4):

---

not clear from Becatti's orientation of the symbol. I have done the same to inscription 3, to give the inscription symmetry between its left and right halves.

6. See Bakker's website at http://www.ostia-antica.org/regio2/4/4-2.htm. Excluding the figures to the right of Becatti's chart and the figures that are interpreted in paragraphs below, the symbols include: (1) two occurrences of the Greek letter chi, the first letter in the Greek word Χριστός (used once in combination with the letter *I*, which could reference the name "Jesus," either as the first letter in the Latin *Iesus* or the first letter in the Greek word Ἰησοῦς); (2) a goblet (eucharistic?) with the letter *I* ("Jesus"?) above it; (3) a phoenix, symbolizing resurrection, next to the letter *R* (*resurrectionis*?); and (4) two double circles—one horizontal with filled centers, one vertical with open centers, which probably represents eternity, just as it later was adopted in mathematical symbol for infinity (∞). (For more on the use of this symbol by pre-Constantinian Christians, see my *The Crosses of Pompeii* [Fortress Press, 2016].) In my view, the symbol near the top right is an attempt to form a snake wrapped around a staff; its form has close analogies to the way this symbol is formed on ancient rings. This does not mean it is not being used as a Christian symbol, however; used in association with the healer deity Asklepion, it might well have been deemed applicable to Jesus Christ as an assimilated symbol.

1. *I* (a single stroke)
2. *E* (two vertical strokes, connected to the *I* by a horizontal line above the three vertical strokes)
3. *S* (in the middle)
4. *U* (beneath the middle *S*)
5. *S* (below the middle *S*).

The pattern then repeats from other side with inverse procedures (so that the second U appears upside-down), with the center S doing double duty.

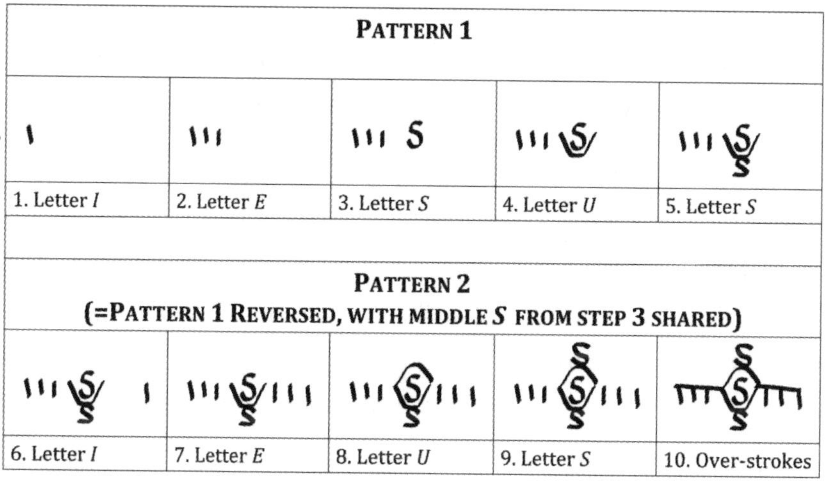

PATTERN 1				
❙	❙❙❙	❙❙❙ *S*	❙❙❙ *S*	❙❙❙ *S*
1. Letter *I*	2. Letter *E*	3. Letter *S*	4. Letter *U*	5. Letter *S*

PATTERN 2 (=PATTERN 1 REVERSED, WITH MIDDLE *S* FROM STEP 3 SHARED)				
❙❙❙ *S*	❙❙❙ *S* ❙❙❙	❙❙❙ *S* ❙❙❙	❙❙❙ *S* ❙❙❙	*S* *S*
6. Letter *I*	7. Letter *E*	8. Letter *U*	9. Letter *S*	10. Over-strokes

Figure 5.4. The Ostian "Iesus" inscription ("inscription 4"), built up stage by stage.

In fact, the same word could have been spelled out in the same cross formation but using slightly different formations for the first two letters. In this option, the letters *I* and *E* lay on their side as a ligature, without the need for an overstrike joining them. In this scenario, two other patterns (patterns 3 and 4) form the name *Iesus* twice, in the shape of the cross (fig. 5.5).

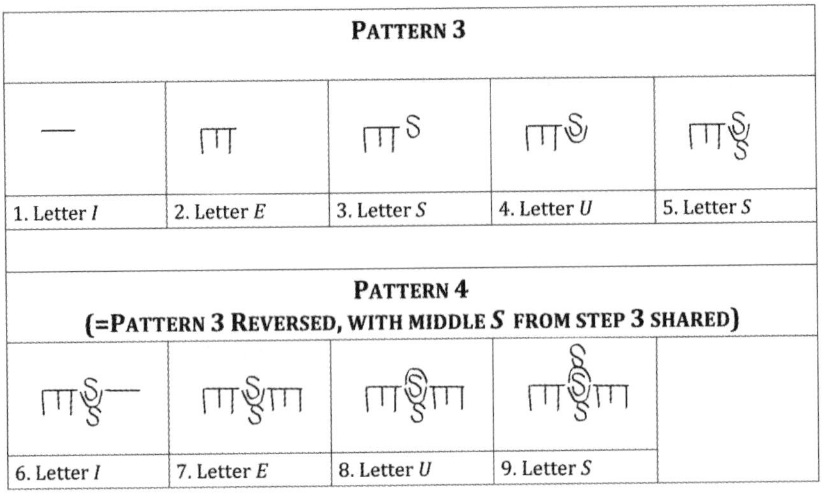

PATTERN 3				
—	⊓⊤	⊓⊤ S	⊓⊤S	⊓⊤S
1. Letter *I*	2. Letter *E*	3. Letter *S*	4. Letter *U*	5. Letter *S*

PATTERN 4 (=PATTERN 3 REVERSED, WITH MIDDLE *S* FROM STEP 3 SHARED)			
⊓⊤S—	⊓⊤S⊓⊤	⊓⊤S⊓⊤	⊓⊤S⊓⊤
6. Letter *I*	7. Letter *E*	8. Letter *U*	9. Letter *S*

Figure 5.5. *An alternative version of the Ostian "Iesus" inscription ("inscription 4"), built up stage by stage.*

Perhaps only the combination of patterns 1 and 2 was intended, or perhaps only the combination of patterns 3 and 4. Perhaps both combinations would have been recognized simultaneously. But despite this uncertainty, we can be sure that the pre-Constantinian Christian who devised this extremely clever inscription was drawn to the shape of the cross as the backbone for his ingenious theological artistry.

The cross also serves as a backbone for other inscriptions in this room, such as inscription 1, the large circular shape in the center of Becatti's lower line of figures. A smaller equilateral cross is also found, slightly tilted, at the top right of that same circular construction. Inscription 2 foregrounds a gamma cross, with the Greek letter gamma (Γ) spiraling out four times from a midpoint, and with one appendage also having a Greek letter rho emerging from it—an attempt to build a staurogram within a gamma cross instead of the usual and more natural T cross. The cross appears also in inscription 3, the square shape next to inscription 1, which seems to combine both an equilateral cross and a chi within a square frame adorned with a circle in its center point.

Evidently, then, the symbols on the floor of room 6 in the Ostian Baths of Neptune include among their number five crosses deriving from Christian devotion (with inscription 1 containing two crosses). In fact, of the various symbols assembled in that location, the cross is the predominant shape. Moreover, these crosses are embedded in quite different structures in each of the five instances. Evidently the cross was the primary shape that undergirded the theological imagination of the Christians who crafted these symbols and who looked for artistic ways of depicting it. Their attachment to and interest in the symbol of the cross appears in the incisions they left behind.

Note also that these crosses were inscribed prior to Constantine. Becatti dates them to "the period in which there had not yet been a full official recognition of the new religion but Christianity had already deeply penetrated Roman society."[7] That would put the date of these symbols in the second half of the third century (like the cross painted in the Aurelii sepulcher) or, perhaps, the very early fourth century. If Christians could be constructing the cross as a symbol in the years prior to Constantine, might they have been doing similar things in generations before that? The material record demonstrates that they were.

The Roman Catacombs

Although it is sometimes said that the cross is absent from Roman Christian catacombs prior to the Constantinian era, in fact crosses

---

7. G. Becatti, *Scavi di Ostia, IV: Mosaici e Pavimenti Marmorei, Vols. I & II* (Rome: Libreria della Stato, 1961), 58–59, my translation (*in un periodo in cui ancora non v'era stato un pieno riconoscimento ufficiale della nuova religione, ma il cristianesimo era gia profondamente infiltrato nella societa romana*).

do make the rare appearance there. In the Lucina catacomb (whose origins date back to the middle of the second century), one Greek inscription appears with the feminine name "Rufina" followed by the word "peace" (much like our phrase "rest in peace"). Below both Greek words, and balanced in the middle of the inscription's horizontal span, is an equilateral cross—much like some of the cross marks on the Jerusalem ossuaries (see fig. 5.6). The most likely date for this inscribed cross is the late second or early third century.[8]

Figure 5.6. The cross in the Rufina inscription.[9]

A cross is also evident in an inscription to another woman whose name appears in the oldest part of the Callistus catacomb in Rome. The inscription comprises the woman's name in Latin letters,

8. See Jack Finegan, *The Archaeology of the New Testament: The Life of Jesus and the Beginning of the Early Church* (Princeton, NJ: Princeton University Press, 1992), 378–79.
9. Ibid., 378.

IRENE, with the symbol of the cross (in the shape of a T cross) inserted between the first *E* and the *N*, being raised halfway above the letters of the name. This inscription has been dated to the second half of the second century.[10]

A fascinating inscription found in the catacomb of Priscilla is also dated to the second half of the second century (see fig. 5.7). The inscription is a beautiful pattern, but what is it? A horizontal trident on steroids? Although some mystery will probably continue to surround this curious inscription, the three vertical lines to the left should not be overlooked. Between them is not a single horizontal line, but three separate lines joined at their ends, as clearly seen at the point where the joining occurs. In other words, these are three vertical lines with their own interlocking crossbars. These are, then, three equilateral crosses found within a Christian catacomb. We will probably never know what the rest of the inscription signifies, but the left of the inscription seems to depict an equilateral cross repeated three times.[11] In fact, they might be the earliest evidence of a ligature commonly used by Christians of the patristic era, with the first vertical line representing a Latin *I* and the second and third representing a Latin *E*—spelling out the first two letters of the name

10. Ibid., 378.
11. Could it be that what we are seeing in the right of the inscription is a combination of three further letters, with the inscription as a whole forming a highly stylized formation of the name *Iesus*? From left to right, the inscription is composed of the following: a single vertical stroke forming a Latin *I*; a double vertical stroke forming a Latin *E* (joined to the *I* by the horizontal bars); then three letters that appear in a stylized ligature—a Greek sigma at the top and bottom (formed as typical lunate sigmas, like a *C*, here elongated) with a Latin *U* between them on its side. Such a stylized formation of the name "Jesus" would make this inscription very much a sibling to the *Iesus* cross found in Room 6 in Ostia's Baths of Neptune (seen in fig. 5.3). The combination of Latin and Greek letters is not standard, however, and might tell against this very tentative interpretation. Nonetheless, as Roger Bagnall notes, inscriptional data frequently demonstrates an overlapping of languages, which were all eligible as "parts of bilingual or multilingual communication and recording systems" (*Everyday Writing in the Greco-Roman East* [Berkeley: University of California Press, 2011], 142). He notes that "some individuals switched easily, even playfully, between them [the languages]," and suggests also that "the disciplinary boundaries usually constructed on the basis of ancient languages serve our studies poorly" (143).

"Jesus" (compare the vertical strokes of inscription 4 from the Neptune Baths, above).[12]

Figure 5.7. Three equilateral crosses incorporated into a catacomb inscription.[13]

Two other crosses need to be mentioned at this point. Although not itself within a Christian catacomb, the first was found "drawn into the wet plaster of an otherwise clearly pagan mausoleum" in the vicinity of the catacomb of Saint Sebastian.[14] There the cross, dating roughly to the year 200, appears alongside the *ichthys* acrostic. Literally meaning "fish," the word *ichthys* was used by some early Christians as an acrostic for "Jesus [*i*] Christ [*ch*], God's Son [*th* and *y*], Savior [*s*]." Evidently one Christian who lived near Rome did not find it awkward for his burial tomb to be situated in a "pagan" location, although he chose to adorn that place with a cross in combination with the *ichthys* acrostic.

---

12. On this, see Paul Corby Finney, "Cross," in *Encyclopedia of Early Christianity*, 2nd ed., ed. Everett Ferguson (New York: Garland, 1997), 304.

13. From Finegan, *Archaeology of the New Testament*, 379.

14. See Peter Lampe's discussion of this in Robin M. Jensen, Peter Lampe, William Tabbernee, and D. H. Williams, "Italy and Environs," in *Early Christianity in Contexts: An Exploration across Cultures and Continents*, ed. William Tabbernee (Grand Rapids: Baker Academic, 2014), 401.

Much the same pertains to another cross in the same vicinity. In the Piazzuola area beneath the catacomb of Saint Sebastian, someone inscribed the word *ichthys* but inserted a T cross into the second position, resulting in the word *itchthys* (or ΙΤΧΘΥΣ)—a formation that is lexically defective even if it was deemed to be theologically significant.[15]

It is also possible that the cross is meant to be referenced in the catacombs through oblique appearances within some of the anchors or tridents that are inscribed there. The anchor is found in some of the earliest of the catacombs (e.g., Domitilla, Calixtus, and Coemetarium majus), including the catacomb of Priscilla, where roughly seventy anchor inscriptions have been found. Especially when depicted with a crossbar or "stock" (i.e., a transverse arm toward the top), the anchor closely simulates a cross.[16] Of course, the anchor might simply have proved popular among Christian catacomb inscriptions because of the close phonetic proximity of the word ἄγκυρα ("anchor") to ἐν κυρίῳ ("in Christ").[17] But even if that linguistic reference were in play, a representational reference might also have been involved in the popularity of the anchor. Debate about whether catacomb anchors referenced the cross of Jesus will no doubt continue for the foreseeable future. For my part, it would be surprising if Christians failed to see a reference to the cross of Jesus in that commonly used shape. Justin Martyr (*First Apology* 55) and Tertullian (*To the Heathen* 1.12) take pains to point out how the cross is recognizable in a variety of ordinary shapes—the mast of a ship, the nose and eyebrows of a human face, etc. If Christians were on the lookout for crosses in mundane articles, it is hard to believe they

---

15. Margherita Guarducci, *Epigraphia Greca* (Rome: 1978), 4:545–47.
16. On the anchor as disguising the cross, see recently S. Mark Heim, "Missing the Cross? Types of the Passion in Early Christian Art," *Contagion: Journal of Violence, Mimesis, and Culture* 11–12 (2006): 184–85.
17. C. A. Kennedy, "Early Christians and the Anchor," *Biblical Archaeologist* 38 (1975): 115–24.

would have failed to spot them in the numerous anchors that they etched into the catacomb walls.[18]

We have seen enough to shy away from the claim that among the pre-Constantinian catacombs "no sign of the cross can be found."[19] They are rare in the catacombs (and perhaps for a reason suggested in chapter 8 below), but they are not absent from that second- and third-century record of the catacombs and their environs.

Christian Rings

In his work on late antique and early Christian gems, Jeffrey Spier takes note of a variety of Christian rings from the third century in which the cross figures prominently. One ring is similar to the *Iesus* inscription from room 6 of the Baths of Neptune in Ostia in that it forms the cross by placing its letters in the shape of a cross. In this case, the cross is formed by means of the Greek word *ichthys* (see fig. 5.8; the three center letters in reverse order would have been correctly imprinted in wax).[20] The five letters of that word appear in the shape of an equilateral cross in this Christian ring from the third century, in which Jesus-devotion is placed front and center.

---

18. An interesting parallel might be the ship drawn by Marcus Julius Crescens in the peristyle of Pompeii's House of Triptolemus (7.7.5). An architect, Crescens found a way to embed his name and profession into the structure of the incised ship, with the first T of *architectus* forming the ship's mast (*CIL* 4.4755).

19. Erich Dinkler, "Comments on the History of the Symbol of the Cross," *Journal for Theology and the Church* 1 (1965): 133.

20. See Spier, *Late Antique and Early Christian Gems*, 184, for the dating of this artifact. He offers no view as to its provenance.

Figure 5.8. A third-century ring with the word ichthys in the shape of the cross.[21]

Five further rings feature the cross (primarily the T cross) together with a Greek chi, signifying the first letter in the Greek word Χριστός, or "Christ" (see fig. 5.9).[22] We have already seen this combination of letters in inscription 3 from the Ostian Baths of Neptune, as noted above (although there an equilateral cross was used instead of a T cross). Moreover, two of these rings share an elaborate two-tiered cross formation (rings 136 and 167, on the right side of fig. 5.9); that is, two crosses appear, one being an equilateral cross conjoined with a chi, above which appears a T cross. In fact, in two of these rings (133 and 136, at the extremities of fig. 5.9) the upper T cross also incorporates a raised Greek letter rho, P, thereby incorporating three theologically symbolic letters and forming a staurogram.[23] Staurograms had entered the realm of

---

21. Courtesy of Jeffrey Spier; also appears in Jeffrey Spier, "The Earliest Christian Art," in *Picturing the Bible: The Earliest Christian Art*, ed. Jeffrey Spier (New Haven, CT: Yale University Press, 2007), cat. no. R3.

22. See ibid., 31, 33. Spier places these five rings into the third century. Ring 133 is "entirely compatible with a date in the second half of the third century"; ring 134 is "typically third century"; ring 135 is "of third century form"; rings 136 and 167 are compatible with rings 133–35.

Christian symbolism before the beginning of the third century (see below), and these two rings seem to be a further reflection of that symbolism, since a mundane use of the staurogram (= the number 3 or 30) is not expected on rings (especially in combination with a chi). The location where these rings were found is unknown except for the one that Spier labeled "134," which originates from Asia Minor.

23. For another crystal-clear example of a third-century chi–rho on a Christian gemstone ring, see Jeffrey Spier, "Late Antique and Early Christian Gems: Some Unpublished Examples," in "*Gems of Heaven*": *Recent Research on Engraved Gemstones in Late Antiquity c. AD 200–600*, ed. Chris Entwistle and Noël Adams (London: British Museum Press, 2011), plate 21.

Figure 5.9. Five third-century Christian rings in which the cross appears in combination with other Greek letters of theological importance within Christianity.[24]

Spier highlights further signet rings in which fish are depicted attached to a cross of some kind (both the T cross and the body cross), and at times with other Christian symbols as well (see fig. 5.10). Closely related to the fish-and-anchor symbol, six of these fish-and-cross symbols appear on rings that have characteristics "which are always of third century date," and most of them are listed as coming from Asia Minor.[25]

Figure 5.10. Two third-century Christian rings in which the cross is coupled with fish.[26]

Two further ring gems link the cross to the symbol of the fish (see fig. 5.11). One (ring 446) depicts a fish above a T cross with

24. The first four are courtesy of Jeffrey Spier and also appear in Spier, "The Earliest Christian Art," cat. nos. 133, 134, 135, and 167. The fifth photograph © 2007 Museum of Fine Arts, Boston, used with permission; also appears in Spier, "The Earliest Christian Art," cat. no. 136.

25. See Spier, *Late Antique and Early Christian Gems*, 47–48. The fact that these cross-with-fish incisions are so much like the anchor-and-fish inscriptions of the catacombs adds weight to the argument that the anchor was likely seen as a representation of the cross.

26. Courtesy of Jeffrey Spier; also appearing in Spier, "The Earliest Christian Art," cat. nos. 269 and 270. See also Spier, "The Earliest Christian Art," cat. nos. 271–73 and 288ter [sic], not shown here.

the inscription "Jesus Savior" below the transept arms of the cross. The other (ring 447) depicts a fish below a body cross, †, on which two doves perch and with the name "Jesus" inscribed twice. Although the find spot for these artifacts is unknown, Spier notes that they are nonetheless "typical of the third century."[27]

Figure 5.11. Two third-century Christian gemstones (one in ring) with the cross linked to the name Jesus and, to the right, the title "savior."[28]

To this catalogue of gems and rings Spier has recently added another third-century ring that he deems to be Christian (see fig.

27. See ibid., 74.
28. Courtesy of Jeffrey Spier; also appearing in Spier, "The Earliest Christian Art," cat. no. 446 (top) and 447 (bottom).

5.12). It interlocks the chi of Χριστός with the tau of the T cross, much like the formation of rings 134 and 135 in figure 5.9 above. This ring originates from Syria.

Figure 5.12. A third-century gem with a T cross interlocked with a chi.[29]

But beyond Asia Minor and Syria, several rings from the Iberian peninsula (e.g., modern-day Spain, Portugal, and Andorra) have been found in Christian tombs depicting typical Christian symbols. So whereas the anchor and fish are found together, so too are the fish and the cross. These rings originate from the third century.[30]

---

29. Courtesy of Jeffrey Spier; also appearing in Spier, "Late Antique and Early Christian Gems: Some Unpublished Examples," in *"Gems of Heaven": Recent Research on Engraved Gemstones in Late Antiquity c. AD 200–600*, ed. Chris Entwistle and Noël Adams (London: British Museum Press, 2011), plate 22.

30. Christopher Haas, "The Caucasus," in *Early Christianity in Contexts*, 127. Note that Clement of Alexandria discussed what is appropriate to include in a Christian signet ring and makes no mention of a cross in either the list of appropriate objects or the list of inappropriate objects (*Paedagogos* 3.59.2). We should probably surmise that the practice of placing crosses in Christian rings emerged primarily in the third century, although we need not assume that Clement

Gnostic Christianity in Alexandria

The second and third centuries saw the production of a number of collections of apocryphal sayings attributed to the risen or "living Jesus" that were refracted through a heavily "gnosticized" interpretative lens.[31] A collection of apocryphal sayings of this kind is found in the *Books of Jeu*. These two books, along with the so-called *Untitled Text*, survive in what is known as the Bruce Codex, a Coptic text from the fifth century that translates a Greek original, dating to the second or early third century.[32] The *Books of Jeu* seem to have had some currency within "gnostic" circles of that earlier period, since there is probable reference to them on two occasions in the third-century gnostic text *Pistis Sophia* (books 99 and 134).[33]

The *Books of Jeu* contain various diagrams that were of critical importance for the gnostic devotee in the process of saving his (or her?) soul from the created order, enabling the soul to return to the high deity as it passes through the snares of the created order. These diagrams are revealed to the gnostic reader as shapes to be reproduced when he (or she?) sheds "this mortal coil" (the physical body) and ascends through the many levels of higher existence, "ensuring the soul's ascent through the various cosmic levels and eventually out

would have known if Christians in Asia Minor had already been making them in the second century.

31. On what used to be called Gnosticism, see Michael Allen Williams, *Rethinking "Gnosticism": An Argument for Dismantling a Dubious Category* (Princeton, NJ: Princeton University Press, 1996); Karen L. King, *What Is Gnosticism?* (Cambridge, MA: Belknap, 2003).

32. This is the date given to the earliest manuscript of the *Books of Jeu* (not extant) by the Bodleian Library at the University of Oxford. See Center for the Study of the Book website, http://www.bodley.ox.ac.uk/csb/OrientalSelectMSS.htm (accessed Nov. 15, 2013).

33. It is now commonplace to recognize that there was no such thing as "Gnosticism" as an overarching system of thought. There were, instead, a number of groups who interpreted Christianity through filters that, in one way or another, can be captured through the adjective "gnostic." That adjective denotes a worldview in which, for the most part, the physical world of creation is inferior to the world of the soul and the knowledge of soul and its true deity. Whenever the adjective "gnostic" is used in this book, it is intended only to signal this general tendency in worldview.

of the realm of Ialdabaoth [the creator deity] and its entry into the transcosmic divine life."[34] The success of one's salvation depended on remembering the knowledge of these shapes, so that they could be reproduced at the proper time, as the soul of the gnostic ascended through the levels of higher existence using these symbols as weapons in the agonistic battle again the aeons. In other words, these shapes were critical to get right.

For that reason, although the Bruce Codex itself derives from the fifth century, the symbols within that codex's *Books of Jeu* are likely to have derived from a much earlier time—the time of the second- or early third-century Greek original that underlies the fifth-century Coptic translation. It would not be in the interests of the gnostic scribe of the fifth century to have changed the symbols, updating them, incorporating new symbols that had no precedent within the earlier Greek manuscript. The symbols represented in the *Books of Jeu* were not like wax figures to be stretched and pulled this way and that way; they were to be preserved and memorized in their entirety, as part of a complicated series of symbols that unlock the various levels of salvation. To adopt a cavalier attitude toward these symbols would be to compromise one's chances of getting through the aeons in the flight to the soul's ultimate salvation from the created order.

It is improbable, then, that the fifth-century scribe would have introduced his manuscript to the group of his coreligionists with brand-new symbols contained within it. We must assume that, in their secret meetings, the group had been collectively memorizing these numerous salvific patterns, learning their intricacies and their sequence, in order to ensure that pattern 52 (for instance) would not inadvertently be used when the soul arrived at aeon 51. The consequences for the soul would have been disastrous. If the patterns

---

34. Birger A. Pearson, *Gnosticism and Christianity in Roman and Coptic Egypt* (New York: T & T Clark, 2004), 267.

from the second-century original manuscript had involved circular shapes, for instance, could the scribe really have got away with replacing them with triangular shapes instead? What about the generations of those who had died already using the older patterns? Had the salvation of the group's immediate forebears been unsuccessful because they had used patterns that were now replaced by others? The situation is very hard to imagine. The simplest and most likely scenario, then, is that the shapes depicted in the Bruce Codex correspond to the shapes already established by the second- or early third-century Greek text of the *Books of Jeu*.

This is important since the cross is a frequently recurring shape (albeit highly stylized) within the *Books of Jeu*. One depiction of the cross appears in chapter 36 of book 1. There a stylized equilateral cross is said to be the symbol that devotees are to seal themselves with in order to pass into the fifty-eighth treasury (see fig. 5.13).

Figure 5.13. The cross as a seal to cross over into the fifty-eighth treasury.[35]

The devotee is given the following instructions regarding the use of this seal of protection:

35. From Carl Schmidt, *The Books of Jeu and the Untitled Text in the Bruce Codex*, trans. Violet MacDermot (Leiden: Brill, 1978), 96.

Hear now at this time the placing of this treasury and all within it. Six places surround it. When you come to this place, seal yourselves with this seal [figure]: This is its name [mystery name]. Say it only once, while this cipher 70122 (?) is in your hand, and say also this name . . . three times, and the watchers and the ranks and the veils are drawn back, until you go to the place of their Father and he gives (you his seal and his name), and you cross over (the gate into his treasury). This now is the placing of this treasury and all those within it.

Later, in chapter 52 of book 2, a simpler equilateral cross is one of the symbols used by those who would travel through the fourteen aeons, outstripping the "archons" who rule over those levels while the mystical souls ascend to the deity of salvation beyond the created order (see fig. 5.14).

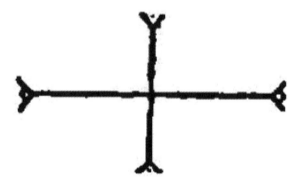

Figure 5.14. The cross as a seal to pass through the fifth of fourteen aeons.[36]

The devotee is instructed to do the following with this symbol:

Seal yourselves with this seal: This is its name: . . . Say it once only. Hold this cipher 5369 in your hands. When you have finished sealing yourselves with this seal and you have said its name once only, say these defenses also: "Withdraw yourselves . . . , . . . , . . . , because I call upon . . ." When you have finished saying these defenses, the archons of the fifth aeon will withdraw and will flee to the west to the left. But you (will) proceed upwards.

36. From Schmidt, *Books of Jeu and the Untitled Text in the Bruce Codex*, 186.

This simple combination of lines in the form of an equilateral cross holds the power to assist the soul in its ascent to the gnostic deity after being released from the body.

More elaborate formations of the cross appear elsewhere in the *Books of Jeu*, serving precisely the same function but at different stages in the progression out of the created order and into the spiritual realms of the true deity. Some of these elaborate crosses appear in figure 5.15.

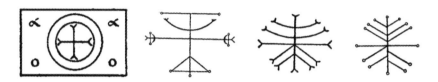

Figure 5.15. Elaborate uses of the symbol of the cross in the Books of Jeu.[37]

These instances of the cross as a symbol of theological importance are a telling indicator about the symbolism of the cross within pre-Constantinian forms of Christianity—in this case, a gnostic form of Christianity. In varying degrees of elaboration, the cross is used as a means to protect the gnostic soul in its journeys out of the arena of the creator deity and back to its spiritual origins.

But if the cross has been transmuted in its symbolic value, it has not been wholly denuded of its connections with the Jesus proclaimed by proto-orthodox circles of Christianity. For instance, after introducing the books as "the teaching in which dwells the whole knowledge," even this gnosticized "living Jesus" offers instructions to his disciples that echo Jesus of Nazareth's command to "take up your cross and follow me" (although here filtered through concepts employed by the

---

37. From Schmidt, *Books of Jeu and the Untitled Text in the Bruce Codex*, 198, 98, 142, 146; see also 184, 190, and beyond.

apostle Paul). So, the very first instruction of the text pertains to the cross.

> "Blessed is he who has crucified the world, and who has not [allowed] the world to crucify him." The apostles answered with one voice, saying, "O Lord, teach us the way to crucify the world, that it may not crucify us, so that we are destroyed and loose our lives." The living Jesus answered, "He who has crucified it is he who has found my word and has fulfilled it according to the will of him who has sent me."

Echoes of the Jesus who died on a Roman cross are still evident, even in this revaluation of crucifixion in a gnostic frame of reference. For the gnostic Christians who treasured the *Books of Jeu*, the cross symbolized their crucifixion to the created order—a central feature of the creational dualism inherent within the worldview of these texts.

This is of notable importance historically, because it enriches our understanding of varieties within the "gnostic" stream of Christianity quite considerably, making that stream more complex and multiform than is often noted. It is sometimes claimed that the cross had no place in gnostic configurations of Christianity. And it clearly was the case that some gnostic Christians took the route of denying that the divine Logos had died on the cross. In their thinking, since the Logos is eternal, only Jesus of Nazareth died on the cross; the eternal Logos must have jumped out of the body of Jesus of Nazareth, perhaps even laughing at those who sought to exterminate him (the view of Cerinthus, evidently).[38] This view is given narrative depiction in the so-called *Gnostic Apocalypse of Peter* from the second century. In chapter 81 of that text, Peter witnesses the crucifixion, seeing things that are not evident to others: "I saw him apparently being seized by them [Jesus's captors]. And I said, 'What am I seeing, O Lord? Is it you yourself whom they take? . . . Who is this one above the cross,

---

38. See, for instance, Greg Carey, *Sinners: Jesus and His Earliest Followers* (Waco, TX: Baylor University Press, 2009), 120–22.

who is glad and laughing? And is it another person whose feet and hands they are hammering?'" Peter is witnessing a person on the cross and the gnostic savior above it, laughing. The savior then says this. "He whom you see above the cross, glad and laughing, is the living Jesus. But he into whose hands and feet they are driving nails is his physical part, which is the substitute. They are putting to shame that which is in his likeness. But look at him and me."

Here the *Gnostic Apocalypse of Peter* adopts what might have been a standard posture toward the crucifixion of Jesus among many gnostic Christians of the second century. But judging by the *Books of Jeu* (and other evidence, as we will see in chapter 8 below), some other gnostic Christians went a different route, giving the cross meaning within a gnostic frame of reference. In this strategy, the cross became a symbol promoting powerful ascent past the aeons as souls find their way out of created order devised by a lesser deity. The *Books of Jeu*, therefore, testify to a divergent appreciation of the cross in gnostic circles of the second and third century.[39]

This couples nicely with the view of Tabbernee and others that the third-century Aurelii sepulcher in Rome (mentioned above) was constructed by a group of Christians who were "eclectic syncretists" and "did not belong to mainstream Christianity"; according to Tabbernee, while it is "unlikely that they were Montanists," it is "likely that they were Gnostics" of some kind ("Orphites? Carpocratians? Valentinians?").[40] As we have seen, this group of Christians included the cross as a religious symbol within a sepulcher painting, with one male pointing directly at a cross.[41]

---

39. Pearson, *Gnosticism and Christianity in Roman and Coptic Egypt*, 267, writes: "the evidence for Gnostic iconography is very meager, but, such as it is, it provides illustrations of the religious experience of adherents of the Gnostic religion in the Roman and Coptic periods."

40. Tabbernee, *Montanist Inscriptions and Testimonia*, 131.

41. The sepulcher, then, was not a place to house the body for resurrection; instead, it functioned as a standard ancient memorial or tomb—a memorial to the departed and a place in which the remaining family and friends communed with the spirits of the departed.

Quite simply, then, some second- and/or third-century gnostic Christians embedded the cross as a theological symbol within their soteriological system.[42] That alone is significant. But there may be more to it than that. Gnostic use of the cross might further indicate the use of the cross as a symbol within proto-orthodox circles of Christianity. If proto-orthodox Christians were not already making use of the cross as a symbol, then the origin of the symbol would be credited to some gnostic circles of pre-Constantinian Christianity (as reflected in the *Books of Jeu*), an invention that quickly found its way into proto-orthodox forms of Christianity as a derivative of the gnostic invention. That scenario is possible, of course, but it strikes me as unlikely—not least when the full scope of data is in view. The cross was too firmly embedded in the theologizing of proto-orthodox Chrisitianities and (as we have already seen and will see further) in material objects reflecting their devotion to a crucified deity. The more likely scenario, then, is that gnostic Christians adopted a symbol from their proto-orthodox contemporaries. Of course, the symbol of the cross clearly meant something different to gnostic Christians than to proto-orthodox Christians in the late second or third century. But what we are probably seeing in the *Books of Jeu* is the attempt to make sense of the cross as a symbol within a gnostic frame of reference in a way that counters the use of that same symbol within proto-orthodox circles of pre-Constantinian Christianity.

The Bloodstone Gem Amulet

The British Museum holds a bloodstone gem that served an apotropaic purpose—that is, it was used as a means of warding off

---

42. Here we can compare the *Gospel of Peter,* in which a personified cross is endowed with spiritual power. A positive appraisal of Jesus's crucifixion on the cross is evident in Valentinus; so David Brakker, *The Gnostics: Myth, Ritual, and Diversity in Early Christianity* (Cambridge, MA: Harvard University Press, 2010), 102.

evil and keeping malignant spiritual forces at bay (see fig. 5.16). Discovered in Gaza, this magical amulet depicts a naked man hanging from a cross. The figure represented on it is the Christian crucified Lord, as evidenced by the words "Son," "Father," and "Jesus Christ" inscribed onto the stone, along with the name "Emmanuel," a name applied to Jesus in the New Testament (Matt. 1:23, drawing on Isa. 7:14).

Figure 5.16. The bloodstone gem apotropaion, with Jesus on the cross as the central image.[43]

Also incised into the gem are several Egyptian magical words used to assist the potency of the magic being pronounced by the user of the amulet (*Badetophoth; Satraperkmeph*). This mixture of religious traditions is not exceptional for amulets, which frequently intersected the various and often fluid religious traditions, drawing

43. Photo © Trustees of the British Museum, used by permission; inv. MME 1986.05-01.1.

"indiscriminately" (we might say in hindsight) on their resources for magical purposes.

In 1981 Josef Engemann charged that this amulet was crafted by modern forgers—a view substantiated only on the basis that depictions of Christ crucified do not appear in Christian art until the Constantinian era.[44] But the charge carries no weight, failing to do justice to the dramatic depiction of crucifixion evidenced within the gem. In 1968 a first-century ossuary was discovered in Jerusalem that contained the bones of a man named Yehohanan whose ankle was intact with a nail driven through it and wooden fragments attached at both ends of the iron. There was no sign of nails having penetrated the arms of the victim, suggesting that his arms had been tied to the crossbeam. Evidently, Yehohanan was crucified with his legs straddling the vertical shank or stave of the cross, as nails pierced his ankles from the sides, while his arms were tied to the horizontal beam (see fig. 5.17 for a reconstruction of the method). This form of crucifixion had no currency in popular, artistic, or academic reconstructions of Roman crucifixion prior to 1985, when this crucifixion position was first reported in an important article by Joseph Zias and Eliezer Sekeles.[45] Nonetheless, this apotropaic gem, which had first came to public light in 1964, conformed to the evidence found within the Yehohanan ossuary—with legs straddling the cross.[46] The crafter of this gem was not, then, a modern forger; instead, the gem's crafter was acquainted with the ancient procedures of crucifixion because he himself was an ancient.[47]

44. Josef Englemann, "Glyptic," *Reallexikon für Antike und Christentum* 11 (1981): 270–313.
45. Joseph Zias and Eliezer Sekeles, "The Crucified Man from Giv'at ha-Mivtar: A Reappraisal," *Israel Exploration Journal* 35 (1985): 22–27; see also Hershel Shanks, "New Analysis of the Crucified Man," *Biblical Archaeology Review* (November–December 1985): 20–21.
46. For the first discussion of the apotropaic gem, see Philippe Derchain, "Die älteste Darstellung des Gekreuzigten auf einer magischen Gemme des 3. (?) Jahrhunderts," in *Christentum am Nil*, ed. K. Wessel (Recklinghausen: Bongers, 1964), 109–13.

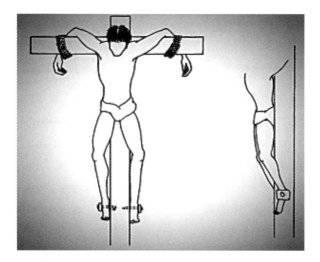

Figure 5.17. Example of one form of ancient crucifixion, with heels nailed to either side of the vertical beam.[48]

The ancient amulet has recently been dated by Felicity Harley (later writing as Harley-McGowan) and Jeffrey Spier to the late second or early third century. They note the following: "The style of carving, material, and inscription are all typical of the large group of Greco-Roman magical amulets originating in Egypt and Syria that were used widely in the Roman Empire during the second and third centuries."[49]

---

47. The same point can be made for the depiction of Jesus's arms hanging from ropes, his naked body, his heavy beard, the profile view of his head—all features that have little currency in depictions of Jesus's crucifixion throughout the centuries. For the profile view of the head, compare the Alexamenos inscription from the early third century.

48. From Joseph Zias and Eliezer Sekeles. "The Crucified Man from Giv'at ha-Mivtar: A Reappraisal," *Israel Exploration Journal* 35 (1985): 27.

49. Harley and Spier, "Magical Amulet with the Crucifixion," 228. They list the artifact in this way: "Eastern Mediterranean (Syria?), late 2nd–3rd century." Notice too that Harley dates this amulet much earlier than the carnelian intaglio with which it is sometimes compared, in which Jesus is depicted as crucified in the midst of the twelve apostles who stand around him, half his size. The intaglio's depiction of Jesus resonates with "images found on a series of Roman sarcophagi of the later fourth century" (229). She dates the intaglio to the mid-fourth century, unlike the late second- or early third-century amulet. Spier allows the carnelian intaglio to be dated slightly earlier, but still within the fourth century (*Late Antique and Early Christian Gems*, 74).

Harley and Spier also note the potential utility of an amulet depicting Jesus and his cross: "The image of the crucified Christ may . . . have been employed by a pagan magician, who borrowed what he perceived as a symbol of great power. . . . The Crucifixion, Jesus's triumph over death itself, was regarded as a powerful symbol."[50] Notice that there is no sense here that the crucifixion must have been a shameful symbol to be avoided at all costs. Just the opposite is postulated. The Christian claim that Jesus overcame death shifted the cross from being a symbol of shame to being a symbol of apotropaic power for use even by those whose religious allegiance was not restricted to a monotheistic form of Christianity.

Should we imagine that this apotropaic gem is the first of its kind, a solitary exception that tests the general rule? According to Harley and Spier, this is unlikely. As they note: "The appearance of the Crucifixion on a gem of such an early date suggests that pictures of the subject (now lost) may have been widespread even in the late second or early third century, most likely in conventional Christian contexts."[51] If they are right, this amulet testifies to the existence of artistic depictions of Jesus on a cross in the late second or early third century across a wide geographical region. Spier makes the point in an earlier publication in this way, drawing on both this amulet gemstone and the Alexamenos inscription:

> The image of the Crucified Christ . . . likely derives from a very early Christian prototype. . . . The magical gem and the [Alexamenos] graffito from Rome suggest a pagan awareness of both the significance of the Crucifixion (at least in terms of a powerful, efficacious symbol) and Christian pictorial representations of it by the third century.[52]

---

50. Harley and Spier, "Magical Amulet with the Crucifixion," 228–29. See also David W. Chapman, *Ancient Jewish and Christian Perceptions of Crucifixion* (Grand Rapids: Baker Academic, 2008), 182–85.

51. Harley and Spier, "Magical Amulet with the Crucifixion," 229.

52. Spier, *Late Antique and Early Christian Gems*, 75.

To be "widespread even in the late second or early third century" implies that this "powerful, efficacious symbol" has its roots even earlier—on a conservative estimate, by the mid-second century at least, perhaps even earlier. As we will see, their view is confirmed by other material and literary data (see, for instance, the dating of the staurogram, below).

Also worthy of consideration in this regard is a jasper gem found in Jerusalem. Greek letters are engraved into both sides of it, probably representing words of magical import. The jasper gem depicts a naked man evidently holding a cross. In 2012, Leah di Segni identified it as a "Gnostic gem," probably used to ward off evil.[53] In 1922, Peter Thomsen dated this jasper gem to the second century.[54] If this gem depicts Jesus holding his cross, Thomsen's dating would fit nicely with the dating of the bloodstone gem, with its depiction of a naked Jesus on a cross and with apotropaic words engraved on both sides. The similarities are striking. Di Segni suggests, however, that "if the cross-like object really is meant to represent a cross," this would make it a Christian artifact (from a gnostic Christian environment), forcing us to date it "not earlier than the 4 c. [fourth century]." Her explanation travels a route that we have already seen to be problematic. The fact that the jasper and the bloodstone gems share notable resemblances suggests that Thomsen's dating is to be preferred. If di Segni is right to identify the jasper gem as deriving from a gnostic context, this too coheres with the gnostic use of the cross noted above.

---

53. Leah di Segni, "Engraved Gem with Greek Magic(?) Inscription, Late Roman (?)," in *Corpus Inscriptionum Iudaeae/Palaestinae*, vol. 1.2, *Jerusalem, Part 2: 705–1120*, ed. Hannah M. Cotton et al. (Berlin: de Gruyter, 2012), 69.

54. Peter Thomsen, *Die lateinischen und griechischen Inschriften der Stadt Jerusalem und ihrer nächsten Umgebung* (Leipzig: J. C. Hinrichs, 1922), vol. 1, no. 209.

The Staurogram

Christian scribal practices in the late second and early third century point in precisely the same direction as the bloodstone gem apotropaion. Three of the earliest papyri of New Testament texts from that period incorporate a staurogram at key points, such as the one depicted in figure 5.18. The combination of the Greek tau (T) and rho (P) along a single stave provides a graphic depiction of Jesus crucified on the cross.

Figure 5.18. A reconstruction of the staurogram and its overline as they appear in John 19:31 from manuscript P66; the initial S has been lost from the left side of the manuscript and the two letters of the following word (τα) appear on the right side of this reconstruction.

Early Christian usage of this symbol is found in three papyrus manuscripts from the late second or, more likely, the early third century: P46, P66, and P75.[55] Figure 5.19 shows a transcription of

55. The dating of P66 is indicative of current scholarly estimates. For a date in the middle of the second century, see Philip W. Comfort and David P. Barnett, *The Text of the Earliest New Testament Manuscripts* (Wheaton, IL: Tyndale House, 1999), 376; for a date "ca. 200," see Barbara Aland et al., *Novum Testamentum Graece (New Testament in Greek) (NA28-T)*, 28th rev. ed., Institut für Neutestamentliche Textforschung Münster/Westfalen (Stuttgart: Deutsche Bibelgesellschaft, 2012); for a date in the first half of the third century, see E. G. Turner, *Greek Manuscripts of the Ancient World*, 2nd ed. (London: Institute of Classical Studies, 1987), 108. Brent Nongbri ("The Limits of Palaeographic Dating of Literary Papyri: Some Observations on the Date and Provenance of P. Bodmer II (P66)," *Museum Helveticum* 71 [2014]: 1–35) proposes moving the date back into the fourth century, partially on the basis of the presence of staurograms in P66. This argument will require the redating also of P75 and P46—not insurmountable problems, but hefty loads for a thesis to bear. Moreover, we have seen three

one part of manuscript P66, with five occurrences of the staurogram within the Greek of John 19:15–20. In each instance, the Greek noun σταυρός ("cross") or a form of the Greek verb σταυρεῖν ("crucify") is written without the intervening vowels αυ and with the letter rho superimposed on top of the letter tau to form the shape of a crucified person—Jesus. Moreover, the words in which the staurogram appear all have overlines (not shown here), which are usually thought to signal that they are words of theological importance, being *nomina sacra* or sacred names, such as "God," "Son," "Lord," "Jesus," "Spirit," and the like (although overlined words are sometimes thought simply to signal the contraction of letters, without theological emphasis).

We have already seen other uses of the staurogram elsewhere in third-century artifacts (embedded within the gamma cross in room 6 of Ostia's Baths of Neptune and on two third-century rings). The staurogram also appears on a wall in a burial chamber in Rome dating to a time before 270. The grave was inscribed with the name of the person whose remains were interred with it: Beratio Nicatora. Beneath his name appear a variety of Christian symbols such as an anchor, Jonah, the Good Shepherd, and two occurrences of the staurogram.[56] Unlike the staurograms in early Christian manuscripts, however, these staurograms are self-standing symbols that are not embedded within the Greek word for "cross" or "crucify." At least by the third century, then, the staurogram seems to have existed in Christian circles in two forms—both within the Greek words referring to Jesus's crucifixion and as a stand-alone graphic of Jesus's crucifixion (much like the bloodstone gem).[57]

---

third-century staurograms from data recounted above, which lessens the force of Nongbri's case that the staurogram is likely to be a fourth-century phenomenon within Christianity.

56. See Finegan, *Archaeology of the New Testament*, 354.

57. Larry Hurtado surmises that the stand-alone version derived after the embedded version ("The Date of P66 (P. Bodmer II): Nongbri's New Argument," *Larry Hurtado's Blog*, June 3, 2014, http://larryhurtado.wordpress.com/2014/06/03/the-date-of-p66-p-bodmer-ii-nongbris-

και βασταζων εαυτω τον σʳον εξηλθεν

βασιλεα ει μη καισαρα τοτε ουν
παρεδωκεν αυτον αυτοις ινα
σʳθη οι δε παραλαβοντες
αυτον απηγαγον εις τοπον λεγο
μενον κρανιου· ο λεγεται εβρα
ιστι γολγοθα οπου αυτον εσʳαν χ/·
μετ αυτου αλλους δυο εντευθεν
και εντευθεν μεσον δε τον ĪΣ
εγραψεν δε και τιτλον ο πειλα
τος και εθηκεν επι του σʳου· ην
δε γεγραμμενον ĪΣ ο ναζωραιος
ο βασιλευς των ιουδαιων· τουτον
ουν τον τιτλον πολλοι ανε
γνωσαν των ιουδαιων οτι εγ
γυς ην ο τοπος της πολεως οπου
εσʳθη ο ĪΣ· και ην γεγραμμε

Figure 5.19. A transcription of John 19:15–20 from P66 (with overlines for the staurograms removed).[58]

These appearances of the staurogram in pre-Constantinian manuscripts and artifacts are instances that call into question the commonplace that the cross did not arise in Christian symbolism until the fourth century. Larry Hurtado has repeatedly argued against the commonplace in recent years, echoing the point made by Kurt Aland in 1967 and, significantly, by Erich Dinkler in the same year.

new-argument/#comments), but this is not demonstrable from the full spread of third-century evidence.

58. The phrase placed at the top of the transcription replicates the manuscript itself; a scribe accidentally omitted the phrase from 19:17, so it was added later above the main body of the text.

Hurtado claims that the staurogram in early Christian manuscripts "has significant implications for our views of the history of early Christian piety, and also for the history of Christian iconography/art."[59] He makes the point this way:

> The *tau-rho* represents a visual reference to Jesus' crucifixion about 150 to 200 years earlier than the late-fourth- or fifth-century artifacts that are usually taken by art historians as the earliest depictions of the crucified Jesus. . . . It is unfortunate that a good many historians of early Christian art are not aware of the staurogram . . . and so do not take account of its import . . . [as] a visual/material expression of early Christian faith/piety [that functioned as] a visual reference to the cross of Jesus.[60]

Consequently, the view that the cross served a symbolic role only in the wake of Constantine is, according to Hurtado, "simply incorrect."[61]

The point echoes Robin Jensen's discussion of the staurogram in these early Christian papyri. She finds it to be "a kind of pictogram, the image of a man's head upon a cross," noting that it "seems to be an actual reference to the cross of [Jesus's] crucifixion."[62] The same point was articulated by Erich Dinkler. We have already seen that early on Dinkler argued that it is "absolute dogma" in archaeological studies that "the symbol of the cross makes its first appearance in the age of Constantine."[63] But later Dinkler changed his mind on the

---

59. Larry Hurtado, "The Staurogram," in *The Earliest Christian Artifacts: Manuscripts and Christian Origins* (Grand Rapids: Eerdmans, 2006), 136.

60. Ibid., 152–53.

61. Ibid., 154. See his other studies on this issue: "The Earliest Evidence of an Emerging Christian Material and Visual Culture: The Codex, the Nomina Sacra and the Staurogram," in *Text and Artifact in the Religions of Mediterranean Antiquity: Essays in Honour of Peter Richardson*, ed. Stephen G. Wilson and Michel Desjardins (Waterloo, ON: Wilfrid Laurier University Press, 2000), 271–88; "The Staurogram in Early Christian Manuscripts: The Earliest Visual Reference to the Crucified Jesus?," in *New Testament Manuscripts: Their Texts and Their World*, ed. T. J. Kraus and T. Nicklas (Boston: Brill, 2006), 207–26.

62. Robin Margaret Jensen, *Understanding Early Christian Art* (New York: Routledge, 2000), 138.

63. Dinkler, "Comments on the History of the Symbol of the Cross," 132, the article first having been published in German in 1951, the quotation here being from page 157 of the 1951 article.

matter. That change was precipitated by his subsequent awareness of the staurogram in late second- or early third-century Christian manuscripts. So he suggests that the staurogram demonstrates that "the oldest sign of the cross as Christ's instrument of torture" is to be dated to "the time around 200."[64]

One further implication can be derived from these early staurograms. As Hurtado notes, it is not simply the appearance of the staurogram in these manuscripts from around 200 that is important; it is also the fact that "these examples are unlikely to have been the originating instances."[65] Or as Kurt Aland put it plainly, these manuscripts were "certainly not the first" to include the staurogram.[66] In much the same way that the apotropaic gemstone of the same period testifies to a broader practice of apotropaic usage of the cross of Jesus, so too the appearance of the staurogram in three manuscripts from around 200 probably testifies to a broader appreciation of the cross as a religious symbol within Christianity.

Asia Minor Inscriptions

In chapter 2 above, mention was made of the graves bearing the phrase "Christians for Christians"—a phrase that identified both those who erected the gravestone and the ones buried there. One grave

---

64. Erich Dinkler, *Signum Crucis* (Tübingen: Mohr Siebeck, 1967), 177 ("das älteste Zeichen für das Kreuz als Christi Marterinstrument" is to be dated to "die Zeit um 200"). He also notes "dass älter als jedes 'christliche' Bild, älter als die christianisierte oder auch schöpferisch-christliche Ikonographie, das Zeichen der Christen für das Heilsereignis, für das Kreuz Christi ist." On the use of manuscripts as part of the material record, Dinkler rightly notes: "Gewiss gehören sie zu den literarischen Quellen, aber als Papyrus-Funde sind auch sie 'archäologische' Denkmäler, die durch ihre Texte als von Christen bearbeitet sich ausweisen" (177).

65. Larry Hurtado, "The Staurogram: Earliest Depiction of Jesus' Crucifixion," *Biblical Archaeology Review* 39 (2013). See also David L. Balch, "The Suffering of Isis/Io and Paul's Portrait of Christ Crucified (Gal. 3:1): Frescoes in Pompeian and Roman Houses and in the Temple of Isis in Pompeii," *The Journal of Religion* 83 (2003): 53–55.

66. Kurt Aland, "Bemerkungen zum Alter und Entstehung des Christogramms anhand von Beobachtungen bei P66 und P75," in *Studien zur Überlieferung des Neuen Testaments und seines Textes* (Berlin: de Gruyter, 1967), 177 ("sicher nicht der erste gewesen").

monument of this kind is of particular note. Dating from the late third or very early fourth century (between 290 and 310) and originating from the Upper Tembris Valley in Phrygia, the monument places a body cross front and center within its facade, highlighted by a circular wreath (see fig. 5.20).[67]

Figure 5.20. A Phrygian "Christians for Christians" monument from the second half of the third century.[68]

Graydon Snyder states that "there is little in the way of content to be gleaned" from these "Christians for Christians" monuments.[69]

67. It is tempting to imagine that the cross is also repeated three times at the end of the monument's inscription. Within the words "Christians for Christians," the Greek letter chi (χ) is rotated so that it appears like an equilateral cross, and the same is true for the final word in the inscription, χαριν ("in memory"). So instead of Χρεστιανοι Χρεστιανοις μνημης χαριν (*chrēstianoi chrēstianois mnēmēs charin*), the final four words of the inscription appear as +ρεστιανοι +ρεστιανοις μνημης +αριν (*+rēstianoi +rēstianois mnēmēs +arin*). William M. Calder ("Early-Christian Epitaphs from Phrygia," *Anatolian Studies* 5 [1955]: 35) adopts the view that these are indicators of Christian devotion, on the basis that a few other monuments from the same region testify to the same phenomenon, and most are demonstrably Christian. On balance, however, it seems best to err on the side of caution and, with Tabbernee (*Montanist Inscriptions and Testimonia*, 266) to take all occurrences of this formation as an epigraphical peculiarity.

68. From William M. Calder, "Early-Christian Epitaphs from Phrygia," *Anatolian Studies* 5 (1955), plate 2c.

111

But this is to downplay two important things. First, these tombstones inscribe the names not only of the deceased but also of those who survive them, the dedicants, who explicitly identify themselves as Christians on a public monument. Here again we see the collapse of the view that pre-Constantinian Christians necessarily kept their heads under the parapet out of fear of their contemporaries. Second, the cross is placed front and center on this tombstone—a characteristic shared by a dozen other tombstones that depict the body cross in focal wreaths.[70] These are all recognizably Christian tombstones from the pre-Constantinian era, displaying the phrase "Christians for Christians."[71] Perhaps, then, the Christians named on these monuments would not have agreed that there is "little in the way of content to be gleaned" from these important witnesses to the pre-Constantinian cross.

Other tombstones also qualify for consideration. Still in the Upper Tembris Valley, a memorial tombstone makes mention of someone (whose name is now lost) having been a Christian; dating to the

---

69. Graydon F. Snyder, *Ante pacem: Archaeological Evidence of Church Life before Constantine*, rev. ed. (Macon, GA: Mercer University Press, 2003), 238.

70. See William Tabbernee, "Christian Inscriptions from Phrygia," in *New Documents Illustrating Early Christianity*, ed. G. H. R. Horsley and S. R. Llewellyn (Grand Rapids: Eerdmans, 1978), 209–12 (from the late third or early fourth century), 251–57 (from 290–300), 258–61 (postulated cross, from 305–310), 261–67 (from 305–310), 267–71 (postulated cross, from 305–310), 271–77 (from 290–300), 277–80 (from 300–310), 281–84 (from 300–310), 288–92 (from 285–300), 292–96 (from 295–310), 296–300 (from 300–310), and 300–304 (from 300–310).

71. The older view that these "Christians for Christians " monuments were erected by Montanist Christians (on the basis that only Montanists were bold enough to proclaim their dangerous faith publicly, since only they were eager for martyrdom) is not seen as compelling today. See William Tabbernee, "Asia Minor and Cyprus," in *Early Christianity in Contexts*, 271, as in chapter 3 above; also idem, "Christian Inscriptions from Phrygia"; idem, "Early Montanism and Voluntary Martyrdom," *Colloquium* 17 (1985): 33–44; idem, *Montanist Inscriptions and Testimonia*, 8, 146–50, 160, 162, 171, etc.; idem, *Fake Prophecy and Polluted Sacraments* (Leiden: Brill, 2007), 201–42. Even if the older view were shown to have merit, there is little reason to think that Montanist Christians were the only ones who adopted the cross as a symbol. It would be a difficult case to claim that Montanist adoption of the cross as a symbol was an anomaly among pre-Constantinian Christianities. As Tabbernee notes (*Montanist Inscriptions and Testimonia*, 9), "most symbols were not the exclusive domain of any one Christian group."

period between 285 and 290, this tombstone memorial is marked by what appear to be three crosses at the top—two within separate circles and one between the two circles.[72] Similarly, in another village, a tombstone whose lettering suggests a date in the second half of the third century simply bears the name "Alexandros." Preceding the name is a body cross, openly displayed.[73] From the same town but a generation earlier (243), the front of a white marble funerary altar names its honoree on lines one and two (Aurelios Satorneinos), and immediately after that, on the third line, identifies him as a Christian. About a quarter of the flat-surfaced top of the altar remains intact, comprising only the far right corner of the top of the altar. Inscribed there is a body cross. We might assume that the other three corners of the top surface were similarly adorned with Christian symbols, perhaps even the symbol of the cross. As Tabbernee has demonstrated, "there is little doubt that this particular cross decorated Satorneinos' tombstone from the outset" and that it was embedded there "as a symbol of protection" by someone whom we should place within "mainstream Christianity."[74]

Approximately 40 miles (65 kilometers) north of that tombstone, another was erected around the year 200 in honor of a bishop named Artemidoros (Ἀρτεμιδώρῳ ἐβισκόπῳ [sic]). The tombstone had been commissioned by someone named Deiogas (perhaps Artemidoros's successor as bishop) and was paid for "out of church funds" (ἐκ τοῦ κυριακοῦ). Various patterns surround the center point of the tombstone, which features an equilateral cross centered within a circle and positioned above what appears to be a table. This is commonly interpreted as a eucharistic wreath-loaf sitting on a portable communion table (a common pre-Constantinian feature

72. Tabbernee, *Montanist Inscriptions and Testimonia*, 248–51.
73. See ibid., 161–62.
74. Ibid., 154–61; quotations from 158–59 and 161.

of eucharistic observance). Loaves of this kind "were marked with a deep cross, presumably with a bread stamp, dividing them into quarters for easy breaking and distribution."[75] The tombstone, then, seems to focus on Artemidoros's identity as one who was authorized to preside over the celebration of the Eucharist.

Four further tombstones from the same region have much the same symbols on them—an equilateral cross within a circular object representing eucharistic bread sitting upon a table. One of these was Deiogas's own tombstone, who himself had commissioned Artemidoros's tombstone; another honors Loukios and his mother, Tatia; another honors Asklepiades and Melete, and another has lost the name of its honoree. There is little debate that these four tombstones date to the first quarter of the third century, that they honor Christians, and that they exhibit the symbol of the cross as a central feature of the identity of the departed.[76]

Just as intriguing is another tombstone discovered about 56 miles (90 kilometers) northwest of Hieropolis. In the year 179 or 180, a man named P. Silicius Ulpianus commissioned a tombstone to commemorate Eutyches, his deceased foster brother. This Phrygian tombstone depicts Eutyches with grapes in his left hand and an object marked by a cross in his right hand (see fig. 5.21). A number of scholars find this symbol to be "unambiguously Christian," an artifact of "undoubtedly" Christian origin, whose "relevance and meaning is plain."[77] For in combination with the grapes held in Eutyches's left hand (as he faces outward), what Eutyches may be holding in his

75. Ibid., 65; see 62–66.
76. See ibid., 72–86.
77. The quotations are, respectively, from Tabbernee, "Asia Minor and Cyprus," 269; and Calder, "Early-Christian Epitaphs from Phrygia," 34. Compare also Julia Valeva, "Les tombeaux ornés de croix et des chrismes peints," in *Acta XIII congressus internationalis archaeologiae christianae Split–Poreč (25. 9.–1. 10. 1994)*, ed. N. Cambi and E. Marin (Città del Vaticano: Split, 1998), 762: "[il] est à mon avis chrétienne." Erich Dinkler ("Kreuzzeichen und Kreuz," *Jahrbuch für Antike und Christentum* 5 [1962]: 111) credits it with having an "ungesicherter Bedeutung."

right hand is a eucharistic bread loaf incised with the shape of the cross on it—much like the tombstones of Aremidoros and four other Christian ecclesiastical leaders from 200–225.

Figure 5.21. The Eutyches Tombstone from 179/180.[78]

Of course, this tombstone might simply depict a benefactor who generously gives bread to the masses, so that claims about it being "unambiguously Christian" are excessive. Nonetheless, the double scoring on this loaf looks somewhat out of place when compared to the carbonized bread loaves from Herculaneum and Pompeii and the portraits of bread loaves painted onto the walls of residences of those Greco-Roman towns. Bread loaves in those first-century towns were typically scored into eight sections, occasionally six. Of the one hundred or so loaves found or represented there, none were scored

78. From Calder, "Early-Christian Epitaphs from Phrygia," plate 2b.

into four sections, as in the Eutyches monument (see, for instance, fig. 5.22).

Figure 5.22. A fresco depicting bread distribution, from Pompeii 7.3.30.[79]

While this might simply be an insignificant variation, the unanimity of the Vesuvian record is likely to testify to the economic realities of selling bread loaves in the ancient world. Bread sellers evidently found it preferable to sell loaves that could be divided into eight parts rather than four. Perhaps different appetite levels could be catered to by eight-sectioned loaves more suitably than by four-sectioned loaves; or perhaps mopping up the oil or fish sauce left in one's bowl when lunching at one of the many fast-food providers was better served with an eighth of a loaf than a

79. From Fausto Niccolini, *Le Case ed il Monumenti di Pompei; Volume 3, Part 1* (Naples: 1890), 92; the original is held in the National Archaeological Museum of Naples, inv. 9071.

116

quarter of a loaf. We cannot know for sure, of course, but a loaf with eight (or sometimes six) sections may have provided the seller with flexibility enough to market his wares most effectively. What is most noticeable, then, is the divergence between the lack of a four-sectioned loaf within the Vesuvian record and the presence of a four-sectioned loaf of this tomb. And this divergence is all the more pronounced when we keep in mind the four-sectioned loaves inscribed on the Christian tombstones of five ecclesiastical leaders (i.e., Artemidoros et al.). Historical analogies would seem to tilt the balance in favor of seeing the Eutyches tombstone loaf not as an ordinary loaf of bread for the masses but as a loaf whose scoring reflects something about the symbolic preferences of those for whom it was baked. Christian eyes viewing this tombstone would probably have recognized not ordinary bread but eucharistic bread—bread that bore the symbol of the death of their resurrected Lord.

⋆ ⋆ ⋆

I can make no claim to having exhausted the relevant artifacts in this overview of the material record; other artifacts could no doubt be added to this inventory.[80] But even if this overview is incomplete, it has nonetheless revealed that the cross was a symbol among some pre-Constantinian Christians, perhaps as far back as the mid-second century. At that point in the development of imagery and artistry, the cross may not have been the predominant symbol of Christian devotion, and it may have been more conducive to representation

---

80. For instance, about 56 miles (90 km) southwest of Ancyra, a man named Alexander erected a tombstone for his father Irenaeus. On it was inscribed a tau "in the shape of a small cross" ("in Form eines Kreuzchens" [Marc Waelkens, *Die Kleinasiatischen Türsteine: Typologische und epigraphische Untersuchungen der kleinasiatischen Grabreliefs mit Scheintür* (Mainz am Rhein: Verlag Philipp von Zabern, 1986), 302]), which might point to a "crypto-Christian" marking (so Waelkens) of a Christian who belonged to "a third-century Christian community" (Tabbernee, "Asia Minor and Cyprus," 298).

on personal items (and eucharistic bread) than to architectural representations in public spaces, but it does have a foothold as a notable Christian artifact within the material record of the late second and third centuries.

Moreover, the fact that the cross is not better attested within the material record might simply be attributable to the frailty of the material record itself. As Allyson Everingham Sheckler and Mary Joan Winn Leith have noted, prior to Constantine "a variety of 'bespoke' Christian images in miniature could have been created independently and in diverse locations across the vast Roman Empire with only a few [of those artifacts] . . . making a lasting impact on what, after 312 CE, would become 'official' Christian art."[81] Along similar lines, Jeffrey Spier notes that, of the extant gems from the first centuries of the Common Era, "many times that number must once have existed."[82] The fragmentary nature of the evidence is itself to be factored into any explanation of the pre-Constantinian situation.

Nonetheless, despite the shoddy nature of the evidence, we have seen that the cross had some currency as a symbol of Christian devotion in pre-Constantinian circles—not only in proto-orthodox Christian circles but also in gnostic Christian circles. The fact that representatives within these broader and diverging streams of outlook and practice held to the symbol of the cross is itself instructive regarding the cross's currency prior to Constantine.

It is easy, then, to applaud the efforts of Harley-McGowan, who claimed that her 2011 study was intended "to raise awareness of the evidence" of the "existence of Crucifixion iconography" in the pre-Constantinian record and to point to "manifestations of that existence in art used in magical and Christian contexts." She depicts

---

81. Everingham Sheckler and Mary Joan Winn Leith, "The Crucifixion Conundrum and the Santa Sabina Doors," *Harvard Theological Review* 103 (2010): 74.
82. Spier, *Late Antique and Early Christian Gems*, 11.

her work as "directly challenging that persistent belief that persecuted Christians were too scared or too ashamed to name and depict the subject [of their faith] explicitly."[83] While some Christians may indeed have been too scared or to ashamed to name and depict the subject of their faith explicitly, the material evidence assembled in this chapter suggests that Harley-McGowan's challenge against the persistent consensus was long overdue.

83. Harley-McGowan, "The Constanza Carnelian and the Development of Crucifixion Iconography in Late Antiquity," 220.

6

The Cross in a Pompeii Bakery

It has often been said that the archaeological record shows no trace of Jesus-devotion prior to the last two decades of the second century or so.[1] But that estimate has recently been overthrown by the discovery of Christian inscriptions in the city of Smyrna that date to sometime before the year 125.[2] In this chapter, we will stretch fifty years further back from that, to an artifact found on the wall of a bakery in Pompeii. A rather neglected artifact, it has unappreciated significance for our topic.

Before analyzing the artifact, it needs to be noted that, with its destruction by the eruption of Mount Vesuvius in 79, the town of Pompeii is temporally located within a period whose character is notably different from most others in the pre-Constantinian period.

---

1. See, for instance, Graydon F. Snyder, *Ante pacem: Archaeological Evidence of Church Life before Constantine*, rev. ed. (Macon, GA: Mercer University Press, 2003), 6; Everett Ferguson, *Backgrounds of Early Christianity*, 3rd ed. (Grand Rapids: Eerdmans, 2003), 589.
2. And perhaps by the discovery of a chi-rho on the bottom of what might turn out to be a eucharistic bowl of a small Christian community living on the desolate Yoronisos Island off the coast of Cyprus in the second century. We await further consideration of this artifact by Joan Breton Connelly.

If we have to reckon with the possibility of persecution (whether soft or hard) against Christians at various points within the first three centuries of the Common Era, the material remains from the Vesuvian towns derive from a wholly exceptional time within that time frame.

This, at least, is the impression given by a variety of ancient sources that testify to the point. No historical source suggests that Christians feared for their lives as a consequence of the initiatives of Vespasian, emperor from July 1, 69, to June 23, 79. Just the opposite is the case, in fact. Whereas Melito of Sardis identifies only Nero and Domitian as persecutors (Eusebius, *Ecclesiastical History* 4.26), Tertullian names Vespasian in his list of emperors who did not persecute Christians (*Apology* 5), while Eusebius claims that Vespasian did no harm to Christians during his reign (*Ecclesiastical History* 3.17). The twenty-five-year period between the death of Nero and the alleged persecution of Christians under Domitian in the mid-90s was not remembered as a fearful time for Christians.[3] Even soft persecution may have been quite minimal during this time, at least if Tacitus is right in saying that Nero's persecution of Christians in mid-60s Rome caused sympathy for Christians to flare up in its wake (*Annals* 15.44.5). This does not mean that all was smooth sailing for Jesus-followers during this period, of course. For instance, we know that someone in Pompeii directed a jocular insult at them in an inscription

3. And in fact, if the surviving texts from that period are anything to go by (e.g., the New Testament Gospels, Acts, the deutero-Pauline literature, Hebrews, the Petrine texts), it was a time in which Christians were finding their voice within the empire. No wonder the Gospel of Matthew, written in the 80s, can end with words that imagine Christians taking their faith boldly to their contemporaries (Matt. 28:19–20). At around the same time, the Lukan Gospel was being composed, which Richard Hays depicts in the following fashion (*The Moral Vision of the New Testament: A Contemporary Introduction to New Testament Ethics* [San Francisco: HarperOne, 1996], 134): "Luke's deep confidence in God's providence imparts to the story a positive, robust, *world-affirming* character. . . . The church is not a defensive community withdrawing from an evil world; instead, it acts boldly on the stage of public affairs, commending the gospel in reasoned terms to all persons of goodwill and expecting an open-minded response."

on the wall of "The House of the Christian Inscription" (residence 7.11.11/14), likening them to something like "cruel swans" (*CIL* 4.679). But jocular insults are not necessarily the stuff of hard persecution, and if we take our cues from Tacitus and others, it seems that Vespasian's emperorship (from 69–79 CE) was a period during which early Christianity was able to spawn without much impediment from anxiety.

Accordingly, in one important regard the town of Pompeii offers us a pre-Constantinian context that most resembles the Constantinian world. If the cross gained its strongest foothold as a symbol within the Constantinian world, might it be that the world of Pompeii offers us a precursor to the Constantinian period, with conditions being as optimal as they possibly could be for the cross to emerge as a symbol of Christian devotion?

Artifacts in Question

The sprawling Roman town of Pompeii, covered by volcanic pumice and ash during the explosive eruption of Mount Vesuvius in 79, has slowly been uncovered as archaeologists from the mid-eighteenth century onward have troweled through the debris that encapsulated it and its sister town, Herculaneum. Along the way, some artifacts have been unearthed that have piqued the question, "Is this artifact evidence that Christians once lived here?"

One artifact of this kind was a word-square, in which five five-letter Latin words were cleverly interlocked in a square pattern. If each of the letters are removed from the word-square and redistributed, a double appearance of *Pater Noster* ("Our Father") along with a double appearance of an alpha and an omega can be formed (if the Latin O is interpreted as a Greek omega)—with the double *Pater Noster* aligned in the shape of a single equilateral cross that hinges on the letter N. If this is a Christian artifact, as some have believed, it would add yet another artifact to our survey of crosses of Christian devotion, with this one dated to the middle of the second half of the first century—roughly forty-five years after the crucifixion of Jesus. Nonetheless, since its interpretation remains controversial, no weight will be put on this intriguing word-square in this project.

Another artifact that has attracted some attention is a charcoal inscription that makes mention of Christians (*Christianos*). Discovered in 1862, the charcoal had faded by 1864 to the point where it was virtually imperceptible to the human eye. Fortunately, for approximately two years, archaeologists had studied it and were (eventually) certain that it made reference to Christians. Unfortunately, very little of the surrounding inscription was legible enough to make much sense of it all. So we know it referred to Christians, but we do not quite know what it said about them.[4]

One curious artifact presents itself for consideration here—a stucco panel that hung on the wall of a Pompeii bakery. As we will see, this artifact draws the discussion of the pre-Constantinian cross into the Vesuvian towns in a fascinating way.

The Stucco Panel in Its Environment

A fairly impressive bakery was situated in what archaeologists have labeled insula 6.6 of Pompeii ("insula" roughly meaning "block"). Judging from one inscription (*CIL* 4.138), in the years prior to the eruption the insula was referred to as the Insula Arriana Polliana. It was an extremely impressive insula that was probably owned by Gnaeus Alleius Nigidius Maius, one of Pompeii's high-status elite. The central part of the insula may have functioned as an elite residence (see fig. 6.1), but dotted around the insula's southern ribbon

---

4. This and other artifacts are the focus of my forthcoming book *The Crosses of Pompeii* (Fortress Press) and will not be considered here.

was a series of separate shops and further residences, which seem to have been rental properties that earned money to supplement Maius's income streams (of which there would have been many others for this man of civic prominence).[5]

Figure 6.1. The entrance into the central residence in the Insula Arriana Polliana.[6]

In the southwest corner of the insula stood a bakery complex, whose oven and millstones are still in place today. This was one of about three dozen bakeries that provided bread for the residents of Pompeii. There were three entrances into this rented bakery: entrances 17, 20, and 21 (designated as 6.6.17, 6.6.20, and 6.6.21). Figure 6.2 shows the overhead plan of the bakery and its entrances. Although entrances 18 and 19 appear to be entrances into the bakery, they were, in fact, stairways to upper apartments, with neither the

5. On the rental properties around the main house, see Felix Pirson, "Rented Accommodation at Pompeii: The Insula Arriana Polliana," in *Domestic Space in the Roman World: Pompeii and Beyond*, ed. R. Lawrence and A. Wallace-Hadrill, Supplement Series 22 (Portsmouth, RI: Journal of Roman Archaeology, 1997), 165–81.
6. Photo used with permission of the Ministry of Cultural Heritage, Activities and Tourism—Special Superintendency for Archaeological Heritage of Pompeii, Herculaneum and Stabiae, which prohibits the reproduction or duplication of this image.

stairways nor the upper apartments having survived the blasts of the eruption. The bakery was composed of three sections—a front shop where the baked breads were sold (entered through entrances 20 and 21), a middle section used for various purposes (which could be entered directly by entrance 17), and the back bakery complex (with no entryways of its own; the solid dark area in the plan highlights the oven within this area of the property, with three millstones in front of it).

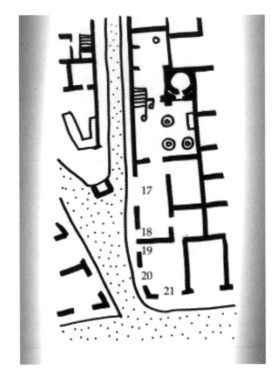

Figure 6.2. The plan of the bakery, with three entrances leading into it (17, 20, and 21).

For our purposes, it is the front section of this bakery that is of primary importance. It was there that archaeologists working under the direction of François Mazois in 1813 found an intriguing artifact. On the wall adjoining entrance 21 and fully viewable through entrance 20 was a stucco panel (see fig. 6.3). The panel included a bas-relief stucco plaster raised within it to form a specific shape. The raised plaster had been highly crafted to form what appeared to be a cross.

Figure 6.3. Looking through entrance 20 into the bakery shop and the wall where the artifact was found.[7]

In the years that followed, the forces of nature removed the stucco panel from its mount on the bakery wall, and today we do not have much physical description of it. Although it was discovered in the days before photography, we nonetheless have a representation of it, carefully drawn by Mazois and included in his archaeological report of 1824 (see fig. 6.4).[8] The bas-relief object fitted squarely within the rectangular stucco frame; there is little room above or below the

7. Photo used with permission of the Ministry of Cultural Heritage, Activities and Tourism—Special Superintendency for Archaeological Heritage of Pompeii, Herculaneum and Stabiae, which prohibits the reproduction or duplication of this image.

object within the stucco, so there is nothing that is missing from the stucco panel. The stucco had been scarred when the top-left-hand corner chipped away, as depicted in Mazois's illustration.

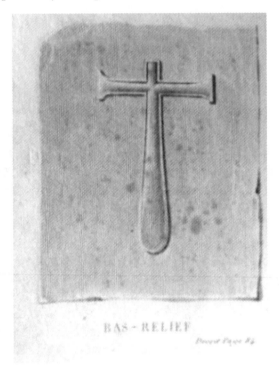

Figure 6.4. Mazois's drawing of the Pompeian stucco bas-relief, with paper mold deterioration causing dark spots to appear on the page.

Previous Interpretations of the Stucco Panel

Mazois was the first to interpret the significance of the raised plaster embedded at the center of the stucco panel. He thought it was

8. François Mazois, *Les Ruines de Pompeii* (Paris: F. Didot, 1824), 2:88. There is no reason to doubt that Mazois's illustration is a reliable reproduction of the artifact's physical appearance, since his illustrations are well known to be accurate representations. See Victoria C. Gardner Coates, "Théodore Chassériau," in *The Last Days of Pompeii: Decadence, Apocalypse, Resurrection*, ed. Victoria C. Gardner Coates, Kenneth Lapatin, and Jon L. Seydl (Los Angeles: The J. Paul Getty Museum, 2012), 100; Richard Brilliant, *Pompeii: AD 79: The Treasure of Rediscovery* (New York: Clarkson N. Potter, 1979), 142.

a Christian cross. Of course, he thought it was bizarre to find a Christian cross in such a place, since some standard "pagan" artifacts were also found in the bakery. Those included, for instance, two paintings of snakes, which represent the spirits protecting the household, and a phallic symbol embedded above the oven to enhance good luck and to protect the product of the household. Could a single dwelling contain images of "the most absurd superstitions of antiquity" alongside a symbol of Christianity, the "new and pure religion"?[9] Mazois was puzzled due to the incompatibility of the material remains—a puzzlement shared by many others in the past, who have therefore denied that the artifact could have a Christian pedigree.[10]

Over and above this perceived incompatibility, a second issue was added to the case against this artifact being a Christian cross: that is, Christians would not have put a symbol of their faith on such public display.[11] This claim was evidently made on the assumption that Christians were always in hiding for fear of persecution. And onto these assumptions, a third is often added—that is, the popular supposition that the cross was not a symbol of Christian faith prior to Constantine. So Graydon Snyder could say as recently as 2003 that if this was a Christian cross, it "came 300 years too soon" since the cross "ought not be considered pre-Constantinian" among the religious symbols of Christianity.[12] (Readers of this book can already see how

---

9. Mazois, *Les Ruines de Pompeii*, 2:102.

10. I will document this further in *The Crosses of Pompeii* (Fortress Press, forthcoming). For now it is enough to cite Marc Monnier, *The Wonders of Pompeii*, translation (New York: Scribner, 1870), 147; Thomas H. Dyer, *Pompeii: Its History, Buildings and Antiquities* (London: George Bell & Sons, 1875), 321; Antonio Varone, *Presenze guidaiche e cristiane a Pompei* (Naples: M. D'Auria Editore, 1979), 31–34.

11. Dyer, *Pompeii: Its History, Buildings and Antiquities*, 321.

12. Snyder, *Ante pacem*, 61 and 14, respectively. It is on this basis that Varone rules out a Christian interpretation of the bakery cross (*Presenze guidaiche e cristiane a Pompei*, 33), along with his view that it is not feasible that Christian piety would appear in a bakery that also displays a phallic symbol.

ill-founded presuppositions have predetermined the interpretation of this artifact.)

For the longest time, however, no one was quite able to explain what the figure in the middle of the stucco panel actually was. What purpose had it served? For some, the answer seemed to come from a discovery first made in 1938, when archaeologists were digging through the ash at Pompeii's upmarket sister town, Herculaneum, some ten miles away. In a small room in an upper apartment in Herculaneum's House of the Bicentenary, another cross-shaped artifact had been embedded within a stucco frame. The object had long since been removed, but its imprint still remained (see fig. 6.5). Could it have been a Christian cross? Many at first thought it was, including leading archaeologists. But an alternative theory soon emerged. The cross-shaped object in the middle of the stucco panel in Herculaneum was determined to be simply a shelf holder, not a religious symbol at all. In the end, the consensus emerged that the Herculaneum "cross" was nothing more than a wall bracket of some kind. And if that was the case, then so too is the cross-shaped object in the stucco panel in the Pompeii bakery. On this view, what hung on the wall of the bakery at the southwest corner of Pompeii's Insula Arriana Polliana was simply a small shelf, not a Christian cross.

Figure 6.5. The cross-shaped imprint from Herculaneum's House of the Bicentenary.[13]

Problems with the Assumptions

Each of the assumptions supporting the "wall bracket" conclusion for the cross-shaped bas-relief in the Pompeii bakery is suspect. We have already seen, for instance, that the symbol of the cross does have a foothold within pre-Constantinian Jesus-devotion; it did not require an age of political power for Christians to have formed the cross within material objects. So the third assumption crumbles.

What about the second assumption, regarding Christians hiding any sign of their devotion rather than placing it on display? We have already seen how precarious that view is—both (1) as a general rule of thumb that is used to demarcate the whole of the pre-Constantinian

13. Photo courtesy of the VRoma Project (www.vroma.org); used with permission of the Ministry of Cultural Heritage, Activities Tourism—Special Superintendency for Archaeological Heritage of Pompeii, Herculaneum and Stabiae, which prohibits the reproduction or duplication of this image.

era in every geographical location, and (2) as a descriptor of the time of Vespasian's reign when, in the aftermath of Nero's persecutions, a sympathetic posture toward Christians was not unknown. Accordingly, the second assumption falters.

But what about the first assumption—the one in which Christians would not have mixed their "new and pure religion" with "the most absurd superstitions of antiquity"? This, ultimately, is little more than a throwback of nineteenth-century piety onto the first-century context. Since nineteenth-century archaeology of Christian artifacts was often conceived as a means of "participation in the society of primitive believers," it was undesirable for an artifact to show "primitive believers" in what was perceived to be an unfavorable light.[14] That is, the archaeology of Christian antiquity was expected to verify the truthfulness of Christianity, the "pure religion." If religious artifacts were discovered from the past, they were either to demonstrate the inferiority of non-Christian religions or were to yoke together "the communion of saints" that transcends the centuries. Archaeology was not supposed to harvest ancient Jesus-devotion that looked like a variation on ancient forms of Greco-Roman superstition, especially so close to Rome, the papal city.

Pompeian scholarship has sometimes referenced "the horror of Saint Paul and the early Christians at the prospect of idolatry" when deciding how to interpret the artifact on the wall of the Pompeii bakery; in light of that "horror" of worshiping objects, the artifact cannot be a Christian cross.[15] But this adds assumption onto assumption. It is not at all clear that the artifact would inevitably be

---

14. On the theological assumptions of "the Roman school" of archaeology and methodological errors that crept in as a consequence, see Snyder, *Ante pacem*, 6–7.

15. Varone, *Presenze guidaiche e cristiane a Pompei*, 33: *l'orrore di S. Paulo e dei primi Cristiani per l'idolatria*. Lurking nearby Varone's interpretations is the issue of whether an interpretation is "in full accord with Paul's meditation on the cross" (*in piena linea con la meditazione paolina circa la croce*, 39).

an object to be worshiped if it were a Christian artifact; discourse in the early church fathers demonstrates a differentiation between the cross as an object of worship versus the cross as assisting Christian devotion toward God (see chapter 7 below). Moreover, as we have seen from the material record and will see further below, crosses of Jesus-devotion often served an apotropaic function in warding off evil—a far cry from serving as an object of worship.

While the apostle Paul might well have appreciated the impulse to separate Christianity from "pagan" influences, the ancient reality was often much different. Syncretism, the mixing of religious traditions, was alive and well in the Greco-Roman world, and Christianity was not always free from it.[16] The bloodstone apotropaic gem discussed in chapter 5 is an obvious case in point. This and many other examples attest to the fact that, all else being equal, Jesus-devotion was occasionally adopted as another form of protection against the harsh realities of Greco-Roman life. Sometimes Jesus-devotion was simply seen as a means to increase a person's prospects (see Acts 8:9–24; 19:11–20); often, devotion to Jesus was not thought to impede one's devotion to other deities (see the issues affecting some of the churches described in Revelation 2–3). As the apostle Paul learned to his great dismay, Jesus-followers in Corinth often configured their Jesus-devotion in ways that illustrated their continuing commitment to practices barely different from those of their contemporaries. In the dangerous first-century world, it might simply have been prudent for someone to add Jesus-devotion to the deities to whom devotion was extended. New Testament authors and leading orthodox figures within Christian circles usually saw things as contrasts of black and white, a perspective that the average Jesus-follower may not always

---

16. Syncretism was adopted even by some Jews; see, for instance, Martin Hengel and Anna Maria Schwemer, *Paul between Damascus and Antioch* (London: SCM Press, 1997), 161–67.

have shared, especially in towns that did not enjoy a robust Christian leadership.

Accordingly, the fact that other forms of religious devotion were attested on the walls of the bakery cannot be allowed to preclude the possibility that some form of Jesus-devotion was practiced in the bakery. The same religious artifact can be used in a variety of different contexts, ranging from religious syncretism to religious exclusivism. Without other data suggesting one context or another, we cannot predetermine in advance how a religious symbol might have functioned in this regard. But predetermination of this sort is exactly what transpires when scholars exclude the possibility that a symbol of Jesus-devotion could have resided in the Pompeii bakery; they have applied an exclusivist category to Jesus-devotion when other options are just as possible.

For these three reasons, then, the artifact in the bakery of the Insula Arriana Polliana has been interpreted within a matrix of assumptions that range from the historically false to the historically dubious. Having peeled back flimsy assumptions, it is time to look again.

Problems with the Analogy

The fact that inappropriate assumptions have dogged the interpretation of the stucco panel does not necessarily require us to accept that it is, therefore, a cross of Jesus-devotion. Instead of a symbolic function, the artifact is regularly thought to have served a structural function, by analogy with the artifact from Herculaneum's House of the Bicentenary: if the Bicentenary artifact was most likely a shelf support of some kind, so too was the bakery artifact. The analogy works on the basis of a similarity in the appearance of the two artifacts (see fig. 6.6).

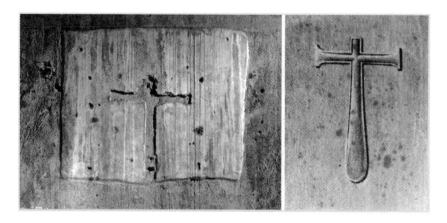

Figure 6.6. The artifact from Herculaneum's House of the Bicentenary (left) together with the artifact from the bakery in Pompeii's Insula Arriana Polliana.

A similarity in appearance, however, is not necessarily an adequate basis for comparing two artifacts if those artifacts diverge in other respects. Most importantly, the construction of the Herculaneum and Pompeii artifacts requires consideration. Could both artifacts have been load bearing? Even if the Herculaneum artifact could have carried the weight of a shelf, the Pompeii artifact quite simply could not. The Herculaneum artifact involves a hard object (usually thought to have been a wooden object) being nailed onto the wall within a plaster panel; the Pompeii artifact was fashioned from raised plaster within a self-contained bas-relief cradle. Unlike the Herculaneum artifact, no nails penetrated the plaster of the Pompeii artifact. It was a self-supporting piece of plaster. Moreover, stucco plaster, raised perhaps a centimeter or so, is not a material of choice for fixing a shelf to a wall; the plaster would simply have fragmented under any noticeable weight added to it, and without a series of nails assisting it, no shelf could have been held there in the first place. When stucco is raised and formed, it is for artistic effect alone, not for structural strength. This must also be the case for the artifact on the wall of this Pompeii bakery.

This point is further highlighted by three features of the Pompeii artifact that suggest not a structural but an artistic function:

1. It flares out at lower portions of the vertical stave before rounding off at the bottom.
2. The horizontal transverse gently expands in width before quickly flaring toward its two endpoints.
3. Except for the tips of the horizontal transverse, a delicate beveling adds an exquisite outline to the whole of the cross.

Are we really to think that these stylistic features were not intended as artistic touches but instead served merely to help support a shelf unit that would inevitably have covered them up? This is highly unlikely.

Consequently, the stucco panel in the Insula Arriana Polliana seems not to have been an anchor or a brace for a wall shelf; instead, it served a symbolic function. If this conclusion is wrong, it will need to be shown (1) how the intricacies of its artistic design could enhance its proposed function as a wall bracket, and (2) how an ancient craftsman could imagine stucco bas-relief as an adequate support for a shelf unit. At present, however, no argument of this kind has yet been made, and it is hard to imagine one being supplied.

Devising a theory about an alleged shared function for both the Herculaneum and Pompeii artifacts requires an explanation that could do adequate justice to the structural features of both artifacts. But the two artifacts have almost nothing in common structurally speaking, and consequently could not have shared the same function if that function was merely structural. Unlike the Herculaneum artifact, the Pompeian artifact could not have served as an anchor for any kind of shelf unit. Instead, it served an artistic function of some kind.

What Kind of Symbolism?

If the stucco artifact in Pompeii's Insula Arriana Polliana served an artistic as opposed to a structural function, what form of artistry are we witnessing?

Agnello Baldi suggested that the artifact might represent a double-headed axe.[17] Proposed in 1964, this interpretation has seen no further supporters. Perhaps this is because the dimensions of the artifact suggest otherwise. The transept arm (which would be functioning as the iron axe head) would need to be far more impressive in its girth and should be rounded at the blade—two standard features of ancient double-headed axes. If the Pompeii artifact were intended to represent a double-headed axe, the craftsman created such a paltry, laughable representation that he would have lost any chance at future commissions from prospective customers.

Similarly, the artifact does not conform to the shape of Egyptian Ankh. It does not display the telltale circular aperture (a handle) at the top of the stave, and neither is there space for one to have fitted within the plaster frame in an aesthetically acceptable fashion.

What other artistic forms present themselves for interpreting the Pompeii artifact? Quite simply, we have run out of viable options. The shape of the artifact does not conform to any recognizable pattern—except one that we have seen repeatedly in chapters above. The only real candidate, or the least improbable possibility, is that what we have on the bakery wall is a highly stylized cross of Jesus-

17. Agnello Baldi, *La Pompei: Giudaico-Cristiana* (Cava de Tirreni: Di Mauro Editore, 1964), 40. He suggested that the vertical stave must be an axe handle (*manubrio di un'ascia*), although he deemed the axe imagery to be a covert way in which a Christian hid his allegiance to this cryptic symbol of Christian faith (*simboli criptocristiani*).

devotion. With its crossbeam just below the top of the vertical stave, this cross conforms to the formation of the body cross, attested in chapter 9 of the *Epistle of Barnabas*. This artifact qualifies as evidence confirming the view of Edinburgh classicist Alastair Small, who wrote the following in 2007: "The evidence for Christianity in Pompeii and Herculaneum is of uneven value, and has been much debated, but when the more dubious arguments are discounted, there remains a residue of archaeological documentation which should leave no doubt that there were Christians in Pompeii before the eruption."[18] This artifact, it seems, is part of that archaeological residue for the presence of Jesus-devotion within the walls of Pompeii.

With that said, however, it is also important to recognize that the cross of Jesus-devotion that once resided on this bakery's wall, while not an Egyptian Ankh itself, nonetheless shows the influence of Ankh-like stylings. Artistic depictions of the Ankh from the ancient world generally fall into one of two categories: simple depictions and stylistic depictions. In simple depictions, the appendages of the Ankh appear as unadorned extensions (see fig. 6.7). In stylistic depictions, however, the Ankh's appendages appear more ornately, with the three linear appendages increasingly expanding the farther away they are from the middle point (see, for instance, fig. 1.7). Further still, this expansion of the appendages commonly involved flaring at the ends, not for the bottom of the stave but for the two horizontal ends. This can be seen in figure 6.8.

---

18. Alastair M. Small, "Urban, Suburban and Rural Religion in the Roman Period," in *The World of Pompeii*, ed. John J. Dobbins and Pedar W. Foss (New York: Routledge, 2007), 194.

Figure 6.7. An example of a simple Ankh, without flaring appendages.[19]

19. Courtesy of Jeffrey Spier; see also Spier, *Late Antique and Early Christian Gems* (Wiesenbaden: Reichert, 2007), cat. no. 665. This is a fifth-century Christian amulet with the cross styled as an Ankh. It bears the inscription "One God" together with the first three letters of the name "Jesus." For a similar Christian depiction of the cross as an Ankh, see Jeffrey Spier, *Late Antique and Early Christian Gems* (Wiesenbaden: Reichert, 2007), no. 664 (left), which was produced in the same workshop. Spier's artifact 664 is inscribed with the words "One God in heaven" and on the amulet's opposite side the scene is of Genesis 22, where Abraham "sacrifices" his son Isaac—a story understood by many Christians to be a christological allegory.

Figure 6.8. An Egyptian painting from the twelfth century BCE depicting two stylized Ankhs (top), with a close-up of the right Ankh (bottom).[20]

20. Inv. 976, the National Archaeological Museum of Naples; used with permission of the Ministry of Cultural Heritage, Activities and Tourism—Special Superintendency for Archaeological

These characteristics of the more stylistic depictions of the Ankh are extremely significant for interpreting the cross of Jesus-devotion in the Pompeii bakery—and in fact, for many Christian crosses from later centuries as well. But keeping our focus within the Vesuvian perimeters, it does not take much to notice the overlap in structural composition between the stylized Ankh and the cross from the Pompeii bakery. Both are characterized by the same two phenomena in the three straight appendages that they share: (1) flared edges at the ends of the horizontal arms, and (2) a progressive expansion in the lower stave.[21]

Accordingly, the formation of the stylistic Ankh seems to have influenced the presentation of the bakery cross. What was once on the wall of the Pompeii bakery was not simply a cross of Jesus-devotion but, in fact, a Christian cross that was crafted to resonate with the formation of the stylized Egyptian Ankh—albeit with the all-important circular appendage at the top of the Ankh being absent (the craftsman leaving no room for its inclusion within the stucco frame).

If this is a notable feature, it is not a wholly surprising one. The Isis cult was alive and well in the Vesuvian towns, with Isis worshiped as a deity who gives to her worshipers vibrant life beyond the expiration of their physical body, thereby enabling them to avoid the murky existence of the spirits of the underworld.[22] While the Isis cult was probably the most popular mystery religion within the walls of

Heritage of Pompeii, Herculaneum and Stabiae, which prohibits the reproduction or duplication of this image.

21. Perhaps the fact that the top of the Ankh expects a circular shape to be appended to it left the artisan of the bakery artifact at a loss as to what to do to the top of his Ankh-like stave: should it flare as well (as in later versions of the Latin cross), or should it simply end? Because the top of the Ankh did not provide a template for the top of the stave, it may be that the artisan chose not to flare that appendage of this Christian cross.

22. On death and resurrection in Egyptian mythology and religion, see John H. Taylor, *Death and the Afterlife in Ancient Egypt* (London: The Trustees of the British Museum [The British Museum Press], 2001).

Pompeii, it is hard to gauge at what point Isis devotion became fashionable in Pompeii. It has been argued that the Isis cult had become "modish under Vespasian" in the final decade of Pompeii's life.[23] Like many other temples in Pompeii, for instance, the temple of Isis had undergone extensive damage during the earthquake of 62 or 63; but unlike some other temples that remained in a state of relative disrepair (e.g., those of Apollo and Venus), the temple of Isis seems to have been fully restored by the time of the eruption in 79. Within the town, portraits and statues of the goddess have been found in a number of Pompeian homes, some of those artifacts having been placed prominently within the house. The prospect of life after death that came to the devotees of the Egyptian goddess Isis had evidently captured the fascination of many within the town.

Against a backdrop of civic fascination with the Isis cult, or "Egyptomania" as it has been called, the Ankh-like styling of the cross of Jesus-devotion in the Pompeii bakery makes good sense.[24] What once resided on the wall of the bakery was a Christian cross styled to reference the Egyptian Ankh, a primary symbol within the popular Isis cult. Whether the referencing was exclusivist or syncretistic we can only surmise. But the similarities of the two cross formations compare well with the ideological similarities of the two religions. The Ankh was the symbol of life, and the Isis cult held out the promise of life after death, while the bakery cross referenced life through a deity whose resurrection overcame death—even death on a cross.

23. Small, "Urban, Suburban and Rural Religion in the Roman Period," 187. See also J. H. W. G. Liebeschuetz, *Continuity and Change in Roman Religion* (Oxford: Oxford University Press, 1996), 180–82.
24. On "Egyptomania in Campania," see Irene Bragantini, "The Cult of Isis and Ancient Egyptomania in Campania," in *Contested Spaces: Houses and Temples in Roman Antiquity and the New Testament*, ed. David L. Balch and Annette Weissenrieder (Tübingen: Mohr Siebeck, 2012), 21–34.

Further

In 2013 Edward Adams noted that "It is generally thought unlikely that the cross was an object of Christian veneration at this time."[25] Here he articulates the consensus view about whether a cross-shaped artifact from the Vesuvian towns could be considered a relic of Jesus-devotion. He is right in his depiction of the consensus, and as we have seen, the consensus is wrong in this instance.

In a forthcoming publication I extend the case that this artifact is a relic of Jesus-devotion in Pompeii, demonstrating that it served primarily an apotropaic function within the bakery. But that demonstration is not required at this point; instead, it is enough simply to have made the case for its character as a symbol of Jesus-devotion within this bustling first-century Roman town. It does need to be noted, however, that there is further evidence of Jesus-devotion from the material remains of Pompeii. Arguing the point will require most of a book in its own right. For now, it is enough to have placed a marker of Jesus-devotion within Pompeii, where Jesus-devotion was represented by at least one cross.

That a cross of Jesus-devotion appears within Pompeii does not require much of a stretch of the imagination, since it lies nicely within a cradle of data on either side of it, temporally speaking. So, for instance, just beyond the date of the eruption of Vesuvius in 79 we find some of the earliest witnesses to the cross as a Christian symbol: the Johannine Apocalypse, the *Epistle of Barnabas,* the *Odes of Solomon,* and *5 Ezra* (the first two of these having been noted in chapter 4 above, the latter two being noted in chapter 7 below).

Evidence from the period prior to the eruption of Vesuvius can also be considered in this regard. The eruption of Vesuvius lies roughly

---

25. Edward Adams, *The Earliest Christian Meeting Places: Almost Exclusively Houses?* (New York: Bloomsbury T & T Clark, 2013), 109.

halfway (temporally speaking) between the Johannine Apocalypse and the end of the ministry of the apostle Paul, who died at some point in the 60s. This was the apostle who, as we have seen, characterized his public message as the proclamation of "Christ crucified" (1 Cor. 1:23; 2:2), and who claimed that his preaching involved the reconstruction of Christ crucified in vivid display (Gal. 3:1). Evidently Paul dramatically enacted and/or vividly described the crucifixion of Jesus when he presented his gospel, capturing the imagination of his audience. This is the same Paul who, according to Acts 28:13–14, resided for seven days with Jesus-followers in Puteoli, about 20 miles or so away from the Vesuvian towns (Herculaneum, about 15 miles on ancient roads; Pompeii, about 22 miles). It is hard not to imagine Paul proclaiming his gospel publicly during that week, depicting the crucifixion of Jesus on a cross in graphic detail (either physically or verbally) as part of that proclamation.

The question, then, naturally arises: Does this cross of Jesus-devotion reflect an indigenous development, something that arose only within the town walls of Pompeii, or might it trace its lineage to a Jesus-group beyond Pompeii, from which Jesus-devotion in Pompeii may have spawned? Here we can only register hypotheses.

Perhaps Jesus-devotion in Pompeii was an overspill from Christian groups in Puteoli. Michael Ramsay notes that the Jesus-movement may have been established within Puteoli as a result of the city's position as a primary point of intersection in the web of intra-Mediterranean travel, where influences of all kinds merged and converged. In this regard, Ramsay includes Puteoli in his short list of cities (such as Corinth, Ephesus, and Syrian Antioch) that "became centres from which Christianity radiated."[26]

---

26. William M. Ramsay, *St Paul the Traveller and the Roman Citizen* (London: Hodder & Stoughton, 1895), 346.

Or perhaps Jesus-devotion in Pompeii was an overspill from Christian groups in Rome.[27] We know that communities of Jesus-followers were based in Rome when Paul wrote to them in 57 (see the various communities greeted in Romans 16).[28] If Robert Jewett is overly generous when he estimates that Jesus-groups in Rome "had grown to several thousand adherents by the summer of 64," their numbers nonetheless had probably swelled to somewhere in the mid- to high hundreds.[29] And among Roman Jesus-followers were important figures in the early Jesus-movement and people who had connections with Paul. Andronicus and Junia, for instance, are identified by Paul as "prominent among the apostles," having been Jesus-followers before he was and perhaps even having been imprisoned with him at some point (depending on how we read Rom. 16:7). So too Prisca and Aquila were highly significant associates of Paul in the spread of the Christian gospel, having resided with him in both Corinth (50–51) and Ephesus (53–55); by the time Paul wrote to Christians in Rome (57), they were living there once again (Rom. 16:3–4).[30] Accordingly, not only was Christianity taking root in Rome; it also had some prominent figures within it, two of whom had been long-standing associates of Paul and two of whom may even have been imprisoned with him, the proclaimer of the cross.

27. Perhaps the presence of Jesus-followers in Pompeii was an overspill from Rome through Puteoli. This option presents itself not least since Puteoli remained one of Rome's main ports, even more so than Ostia, up to the time of Nero. On this, see Peter Lampe, *From Paul to Valentinius: Christians at Rome in the First Two Centuries* (Minneapolis: Fortress Press, 2003), 10.

28. On Romans 16 as an integral part of the letter to the Romans (in contrast to other theories about its provenance), see Bruce Longenecker and Todd Still, *Thinking through Paul: A Survey of His Life, Letters, and Theology* (Grand Rapids: Zondervan, 2014), 165–66.

29. This calculation is based on Robert Jewett's arguments for a sizable number (*Romans: A Commentary* [Minneapolis: Fortress Press, 2006], 61–62), without adopting what looks to me like an overblown figure of "several thousand."

30. Departing Rome, Prisca and Aquila relocated in Corinth (Acts 18:2) and then moved to Ephesus (1 Cor. 16:19, written from that city), before returning to Rome, evidently after the death of Claudius in 54.

Moreover, Christians from Rome might have spilled out from the imperial city during the 60s. Christians had already left Rome in 49, when Claudius's expulsion of the Jews had the effect of ejecting Jewish Christians from Rome—such as Prisca and Aquila (Acts 18:2), who returned to Rome sometime after Claudius's death in 54, when his edict was no longer in effect (Rom 16:3). A similar move out of Rome to other urban centers is probable during the mid-60s, when Nero was persecuting Christians.[31] Some Jesus-followers in Rome must have managed to evade the atrocities by fleeing the city.[32] We cannot exclude the possibility that some went south on the Italian peninsula, perhaps arriving in the town of Pompeii. As Lampe notes, "earliest Christianity spread along routes that Judaism had already followed,"[33] and a Jewish presence is evident in Pompeii and the surrounding region at this time.[34]

31. The reference to Aquila and Prisca in 2 Tim. 4:19 suggests that they fled the city a second time. This inference is probably applicable regardless of whether the text was penned by Paul himself or by someone after Paul's death.

32. So Jewett, *Romans*, 62.

33. Lampe, *From Paul to Valentinus*, 9. The point is questioned by Simon Price, "Religious Mobility in the Roman Empire," *Journal of Roman Studies* 96 (2006): 12–13.

34. Small ("Urban, Suburban and Rural Religion in the Roman Period," 195) notes that "Jews are well attested at Pompeii." See especially *CIL* 4.5244; 4.4976; 4.6990; and the painting of the judgment of Solomon in 1 Kings 3 (from 7.5.24, although the relevance of this painting to this issue is disputed). Other proposed data is much less secure, especially the attempt to reconstruct Hebrew names from Latin equivalents, as is frequently attempted by Carlo Giordano and Isidoro Kahn, *The Jews in Pompeii, Herculaneum, Stabiae and in the Cities of Campania Felix*, 3rd ed., trans. Wilhelmina F. Jashemski (Rome: Bardi Editore, 2001). The name "Maria" has frequently been thought to be a Jewish name, although it could simply be the feminine form of Marius. Amphorae marked *garum castum* might well have signaled "kosher garum" for a Jewish population (*CIL* 4.2569, 2611, 5660–62), but there are other options that make that identification problematic. See Robert I. Curtis, "The Garum Debate: Was There a Kosher Roman Delicacy at Pompeii?," *Biblical Archaeological Society: Bible History Daily* (blog), January 25, 2012, http://www.biblicalarchaeology.org/daily/archaeology-today/biblical-archaeology-topics/the-garum-debate/. The presence of Jews in Puteoli is testified to by Josephus (*Jewish War* 2.104; *Jewish Antiquities* 17.328). Josephus also tells us of two people who died in the eruption of Vesuvius, and at least one had Jewish identity or heritage (*Jewish Antiquities* 20:141-144). He was Agrippa, the son of Felix and Drusilla (a Jewish woman), the other was Agrippa's wife, whose name is not known. According to Acts 23:12-24:27, Felix was the Roman procurator who heard Paul's defense in Jerusalem and conversed with him "very often" (24:26).

Whether through Neronian persecution or simple changes in location, it does not involve a stretch of the imagination to envisage some Jesus-followers in Rome dispersing out into other urban centers, perhaps including Pompeii. Tacitus, the early second-century Roman historian, seems to describe Rome as an important base for the spread of the early Jesus-movement when he wrote the following (*Annals* 15.44): "Nero fastened the guilt [for the burning of Rome in 64] and inflicted the most exquisite tortures on a class hated for their abominations, called Christians by the populace . . . a most mischievous superstition . . . [that] broke out not only in Judea, the first source of the evil, *but even in Rome*" (emphasis added).

With Rome being one of the main cities from which the "mischievous superstition" spread, it is not hard to imagine that city having spawned Jesus-groups elsewhere within Italy itself.[35] According to Ignatius, Christians at Rome were well known to have "taught others" (Ignatius, *To the Romans* 3.1). This is testified to by *1 Clement* from the late first or early second century, a letter from a Christian in Rome to Christians in Corinth. The author of that text displays intricate knowledge of the situation facing Corinthian Christians and takes the opportunity to instruct them extensively.

Ultimately, we will never be able to trace the DNA of Jesus-devotion from the Insula Arriana Polliana to Jesus-groups beyond Pompeii. The initiative of depicting the cross of Jesus in an artistic medium might have been a wholly indigenous articulation of

35. We cannot be sure whether the spread of Jesus-devotion into Pompeii would have happened before or after 60. Luke says nothing of Jesus-followers in the Vesuvian towns when recounting Paul's voyage to Rome in the year 60, but since it was not his intention to recount Italian locations where Jesus-followers were embedded, this is an irrelevant silence. Even if it could somehow be demonstrated that Jesus-followers were absent from Pompeii in the early 60s, we seem to have evidence of their presence in that town not long after that. If it took the Jesus-movement less than thirty years to spread 130 miles from Rome to Puteoli (or from Judaea to Puteoli, if that much larger distance is how things happened), then spreading a further 20 miles from Puteoli to Pompeii in the following fifteen years would not seem out of the ordinary.

religious sentiment that had no precedent, sibling, or further influence beyond the walls of Pompeii. But a DNA of Jesus-devotion is there within that town nonetheless, and it is a Jesus-devotion that foregrounds the symbol of the cross.

The last days of Pompeii are as close as we can get within the pre-Constantinian age to the freedom enjoyed by Christians in the Constantinian era; perhaps those days also give us a foreshadowing of things to come in the Contantinian age, with the cross serving as a symbol of power against forces (here, spiritual; there, political) that were deemed to be detrimental to well-being. It did not take Constantine to manufacture the cross as a symbol of Christian devotion. The cross was visually embedded within the Jesus-devotion of Pompeii (and perhaps beyond) within the second generation of the early Jesus-movement, when at least one Jesus-devotee in a bakery "left his mark" on the world that mattered.

7

The Cross in the Literary Record

This chapter will survey Christian literary sources of the second and third century (and occasionally the early fourth century) for their relevance in understanding the role of the cross as a symbol of Christian identity in the pre-Constantinian period. It allows us to overlay the literary data onto the material record. Without a material record as a platform, it might be argued that the cross was nothing more than a conceptual trope of theological importance within pre-Constantinian Christianities, a theological construct that had no impact on the material world of Christian artistry. But with the material record undergirding the discussions of these texts, we can recognize them for what they are—discursive evidence that further confirms what the material record has already demonstrated.[1]

To illustrate the point, notice what happens within book 8 of the *Sibylline Oracles*. This book combines a Jewish text (i.e., the first

---

1. No attempt is made to survey everything that was said prior to Constantine about the crucifixion of Jesus. Instead, only the data that pertains to the symbolic function of the cross is assembled here.

half; 1–216) and a Christian text (i.e., the second half; 217–500). The Christian section of the text begins with a title, "Jesus Christ, Son of God, Savior, Cross." With the exception of the word "cross," this arrangement of words corresponds with the *ichthys* acrostic of which early Christians made so much use. We have seen this already in chapter 5 above, where the five letters of the Greek word "fish" (*ichthys*, representing "Jesus Christ, Son of God, Savior") were laid out in the shape of an equilateral cross in a third-century ring. Here in book 8 of the *Sibylline Oracles*, the same combination of words appears, only here they are fully spelled out, not simply contained within an *ichthys* acrostic. Moreover, the unpacked *ichthys* acrostic then goes on to serve as the basis for an elaborate acrostic poem, which is placed immediately after the title. What appears there is a thirty-four-line poem with all the lines starting with successive Greek letters from the title—a title that combines the unpacked *ichthys* acrostic and the word "cross."[2]

This, of course, does not give us a window onto a physical artifact in which the cross is reconstructed, so it will not be included in the overall inventory of pre-Constantinian crosses. It does illustrate, however, that the artisan who crafted this third-century poem thought that the cross was inseparable from reflections on the identity of "Jesus Christ, Son of God, Saviour." (Compare the formation of the word *itchthys* beneath the catacomb of Saint Sebastian, with the cross embedded as the second letter in the word *ichthys,* as noted in chapter 5 above.) The craftsman was not a gem cutter or a ring maker or an amulet inscriber, and consequently he did not leave behind a physical representation of the cross; but he was a wordsmith, and one who thought it only right to place the cross at the forefront of his

2. Normally these words would comprise thirty-three letters, but the word "Christ" has an additional epsilon added before the iota.

craft. Other Christian wordsmiths from the pre-Constantinian period testify to a similar sentiment, as demonstrated in this chapter.

1. Literary Evidence in the First Half of the Third Century

At some point in the first half of the third century, the apocryphal work *Acts of Thomas* depicts the sign of the cross being made over the bread during a eucharistic celebration (50). According to that text from Syria, making the symbol of the cross is not restricted to use in ritual contexts. For instance, when Thomas addresses a young man, the apostle says to him, "Stretch your mind towards our Lord," at which point Thomas "signed him with the cross" (54 [Syriac]). So too, one ancient document credits the early third-century bishop Hippolytus of Rome as describing apostates from the Christian faith as those who had once been "marked with the seal of my cross [notes Jesus]" but who later "deleted it by [their] hardness of heart" (*Appendix to the Works of Hippolytus* 48). Cyprian, who would suffer martyrdom in the Decian persecution, spoke of "the sign of the cross" as a sign of salvation through which victory is ultimately assured; explicitly citing Ezek. 9:4–6, he refers to it as a sign that Christians place on their foreheads (*Testimonies* 2.21–22). This confirms the continuing vibrancy of the tradition that identified two intersecting lines as the "mark" of Ezekiel 9 (precisely the same tradition that appeared at around the same time in Origen's *Selecta in Ezehielem* 9, as noted in chapter 3 above). Elsewhere, Cyprian makes it plain that this "sign of Christ" is the shape of the cross (*To Demetrianus* 22).[3]

Early in the third century, in the city of Carthage in Northern Africa, the theologian Tertullian noted that Christians held to long-established traditions, including Baptism and the Eucharist.

---

3. The placing the sign of the cross on the forehead of those baptized as Christians is mentioned in the *Apostolic Tradition* 21.23, but because the date of this work is uncertain, ranging anywhere from the second to the fourth century, it is left out of consideration here.

Alongside these he also placed the practice of making the sign of the cross on their foreheads (*De Corona* 3, written in 211): "At every forward step and movement, at every going in and out, when we put on our clothes and shoes, when we bathe, when we sit at table, when we light the lamps, on couch, on seat, in all the ordinary actions of daily life, we trace upon the forehead the sign."

Since "the sign" traced "upon the forehead" is, uncontroversially, the sign of the cross, this text testifies that the symbol of the cross was alive and well among ordinary Christians at the beginning of the third century. It was a part of their everyday life, a practice of Christian identity within mundane practices. Moreover, Tertullian believed that making the sign of the cross within "the ordinary actions of daily life" was an extension of a Christian's foundational baptismal identity. Baptism, for Tertullian, included placing the sign of the cross on the "flesh" of the person being baptized: "The flesh, indeed, is washed, in order that the soul may be cleansed; the flesh is anointed that the soul may be consecrated; the flesh is signed [with the cross], that the soul too may be fortified" (*On the Resurrection of the Flesh* 8). Elsewhere Tertullian notes that Baptism "seals" the person for God (*Letters* 73.6.2; cf. 69.2.2), so that "those who are baptized in the church obtain the Holy Spirit and are perfected with the Lord's seal" (*Letters* 73.9.2).

Evidently this practice of placing the sign of the cross on the foreheads of Christians continued to be common among Christians a century later. Lactantius, writing his *Divine Institutes* during Diocletian's near-decade of persecution against Christians from 303 to 311, refers to the cross as a symbol that Christians replicated on their foreheads (*Divine Institutes* XXVI):

> Therefore in His suffering He stretched forth His hands and measured out the world, that even then He might show that a great multitude,

collected together out of all languages and tribes, . . . was about to come under His wings and to receive on their foreheads that great and lofty sign. . . . For Christ . . . is the salvation of all who have written on their foreheads the sign of blood—that is, of the cross, on which He shed His blood. For the forehead is the top of the threshold in man, and the wood sprinkled with blood is the emblem [*significatio*] of the cross.

We might want to say that the examples offered thus far indicate merely the importance of a symbolic gesture among Christians, and give no basis for thinking that Christians depicted the cross visually within artistic media. But while it is important not to overstep the evidence, a coupling of the material and literary evidence suggests that this practical gesture, utilized both in Christian worship services and in daily life, often spilled over onto material realia, where the shape of that temporary gesture is represented in visual artistic form—something that the material record suggests had already been happening before the time of Tertullian.

Of course, besides making gestures at key points throughout their day, Tertullian does not mention that some Christians were also crafting the shape of the cross into tombstones, marking graves with it, or forming it by means of staurograms. But as we have already seen, the material record testifies that these things (and more) were happening, as Christians transferred the image into artistic representation. Tertullian did not intend to provide a complete inventory on all the ways that the cross was being formed and fashioned by Christians of his day. Instead, he was simply speaking of important ecclesiastical traditions that Christians had handed on throughout the generations, like the rites of Baptism and the Eucharist. That he includes cruciform gestures as a third important tradition passed on by generations of Christians should not be taken to imply that no Christian ever thought of crafting a cruciform symbol. In fact, we have seen that some did.

This coincides with Tertullian's comments in *Against Marcion*, written about 207 (although with drafts having been written prior to that date). In *Against Marcion* 3.22, Tertullian comments on Ezek. 9:4, which (as we saw in chapter 3 above) speaks of putting "a mark on the foreheads of those who sigh and groan over all the abominations that are committed" in Jerusalem. Tertullian notes: "Now the Greek letter *Tau* and our own [Latin] letter *T* is the very form of the cross, which He [God] predicted would be the sign on our foreheads in the true Catholic Jerusalem." This visualization of the shape of the cross is significant in two ways. First, it alters the formation of the "mark" of Ezek. 9:4, with the ancient Hebrew letter tav (written as + or x) now morphing into the Greek and Latin T.[4] Second, it adds further confirmation that Christian appreciation of the cross as a theological symbol was a pre-Constantinian phenomenon. As Larry Hurtado notes on the basis of this passage, "the [Greek] *tau* by itself" must have been "an acknowledged visual symbol of Jesus' cross" prior to Tertullian.[5]

Clement of Alexandria, writing around the year 200 in Egypt, referred to the cross as "the Lord's sign" (*Miscellanies* 6.11.87.2; cf. 6.11.84.3).[6] And the cross is depicted as a Christian symbol in the work *Octavius*, written by Marcus Minucius Felix, the little-known Latin Christian apologist who wrote probably in the second half of the second century, or perhaps the beginning of the third century. Minucius Felix felt the need to respond to the criticisms against

4. I am not proposing that Tertullian knew Hebrew; as far as I am aware, there is no sign of this in his extant literature. The point is simply phenomenological; when Tertullian read Ezek. 9:4 and imagined it to be a T cross, the equilateral possibility of the Paleo-Hebrew is nowhere in sight. Tertullian also engages with the "mark" of Ezekiel 9 in *De Adversus Iudeaos* 11, where he speaks of the mark of protection as being "sealed with the passion of the Christ."

5. Larry Hurtado, "The Staurogram: Earliest Depiction of Jesus' Crucifixion," *Biblical Archaeology Review* 39 (2013): 148–49.

6. The point is made that "three hundred cubits are the symbol of the Lord's sign" because 300 is the isopsephic value for the Greek letter T, the shape of a *crux commissa*.

Christianity lodged by a man named Caecilius, who charged that Christians worship a cross (chaps. 9 and 12). Noting how pagans "attribute to our religion the worship of a criminal and his cross," Minucius Felix notes that although the "wood of the cross" was a central feature in the worship practices of Christians (*Octavius* 29.6–8), "crosses are not objects that we worship" (*Octavius* 29).[7] Behind this dispute we glimpse that the cross was a cherished symbol of identity for many Christians, with that symbol being misinterpreted by non-Christians as a central object of their worship. Evidently the cross was firmly embedded within practices of devotion by some Christians known to Minucius Felix.

These five texts, written at the turn of the second to the third century, testify to the cross being an established symbol within Christian circles at that point (coinciding with the findings of chapter 5 above). Even the opponents of Christians are said to have noted this. Moreover, for the practice to have been widespread and ingrained within every aspect of daily life (or so Tertullian would have us believe), the practice must have deeper roots well within the second century, as Tertullian noted. If these texts do not speak of Christian crafting rings with crosses in them and the like, that does not mean that Christians were not doing precisely that. These texts, instead, offer some of the theological rationales for why Christians were doing precisely that.

2. Literary Evidence from the Second Century

Moving back into the second century, the *Acts of Peter* derives from the second half of that century, probably from Asia Minor. In one episode, it purportedly recounts Peter's travels from Caesarea to Rome. When the ship's captain hears Peter's message, he asks to

---

7. On this, note also Tertullian, *To the Heathen* 1.11, which Minucius Felix probably knew.

be baptized "with the sign of the Lord" (*in signo domini*); after the baptisms, several Christians share in the Eucharist, the captain being worthy to participate because, as mentioned in prayer to the "God Jesus Christ," he has been "signed with your holy sign" (*signatus est sancto tuo signo; Acts of Peter* 5).

At about the same time (i.e., a decade or two before 190), the *Acts of Paul and Thecla* recounts the mission of Thecla in service to the Christian gospel. An extremely popular text in its day, the *Acts of Paul and Thecla* recounts one episode in which her persecutors attempt to burn Thecla at the stake. Before the fire is lit, she makes "the sign of the cross" (τὸν τύπον τοῦ σταυροῦ, 5.14). Although a huge fire engulfs the pyre, Thecla is preserved unharmed. In a later episode, she makes "the sign" over the whole of her body (10.10).

The same expression is found earlier, in the work of Justin Martyr from the mid-second century (c. 100–165)—especially his *First Apology* written in 155 or so, and his *Dialogue with Trypho*, written about 160. When considering the success of the Hebrew people in the Old Testament, Justin introduces the cross into his reconstruction of their military battles (cf. Exod. 17:9–14), much like the author of *Epistle of Barnabas* had done a few decades earlier. Here is what Justin says in *Dialogue* 90 regarding a battle between the Hebrew people and their enemies, with Moses and Joshua playing key roles in the battle (the Hebrew name "Joshua" becomes "Jesus" in Greek ['Ιησοῦς]): "For it was not because Moses so prayed that the people were stronger, but because, while one who bore the name of Jesus [Joshua] was in the forefront of the battle, he [Moses] made himself the sign of the cross."

Justin depicts Moses placing his body into a posture that replicated the shape of a cross; with hands outstretched at his sides, "he made himself the sign of the cross." With Moses striking that cruciform pose (and with a "Jesus" at the frontline of the battle), divine favor resulted. Justin prefaced all of this by speaking of the importance of "signs" or symbols that are embedded within scripture and prefigure the Christian gospel.

In *Dialogue* 60 Justin engages in christological interpretation of another incident in Moses's life. He notes the following:

> when the Israelites had gone out of Egypt and were in the wilderness, they encountered poisonous beasts, vipers and asps, and every kind of snake which were killing the people. By an inspiration and influence that came from God, Moses took brass and made the form of a cross, and placed it over the holy tent, saying to the people, "If you look on this form and believe on it, you will be saved." And he records that when this was done, the snakes died, and so, he tells us, the people escaped death.

Here Moses fashions the "form of a cross" out of brass, fixes it to the tabernacle where God's presence dwells with the people, and proclaims that the people should look on this crafted symbol for their salvation. Justin expects his readers to imagine a cross crafted from physical materials as symbol of life-giving power.

There is no reason to think that Justin introduced this symbol of the cross to his audiences; his talk of "the sign of the cross" and "the form of the cross" flows unobtrusively into his discourse, suggesting that Justin expected his Christian readers in Rome and beyond to recognize its symbolic significance in relation to their identity. For Justin's discourse to carry weight with his audience, the symbol of the cross must have had some currency among some Christians in the middle of the second century.

The *Odes of Solomon* also demonstrate that the cross of Christ was being meditated on as an image for the edification of Jesus-devotion from an early date. James Charlesworth has argued that the *Odes of Solomon* is a Christian text that was composed "sometime around A.D. 100."[8] There is scope for putting it slightly later into the second century, but not much later—probably between 110 and 120, making it roughly contemporaneous with the *Epistle of Barnabas*.[9] Most think it to have originated in Syria. Note then how this early second-century Syrian text mentions the cross as the "sign" of Jesus in *Ode* 27: "I extended my hands and hallowed my Lord, for the expansion of my hands is his sign. And my extension is the upright cross. Hallelujah."

The acknowledgement that the formation of the body cross represents "his sign" corresponds also with the early Christian use of the *orans*—a figure standing in prayer, usually female, perhaps representing the soul of the deceased. Artistic depictions of the prayerful *orans* with outstretched arms are frequently found in Christian catacombs of second- and third-century Rome. According to Richard Viladesau, we can deduce from this "that the early Christians stood cruciform in prayer, with arms extended to the side, rather than raised above the head, as was the pagan custom."[10] Although the *oranic* posture is not in itself an "artistic" artifact, the posture itself seems to testify to the fact that the cross was morphing into the physical world of Christian devotion. It was, as Paul Finney notes, "simultaneously a prayer position and a reminder to early Christians of the cross."[11]

---

8. James H. Charlesworth, *The Old Testament Pseudepigrapha* (Garden City, NY: Doubleday, 1985), 2:727. See also idem, *Critical Reflections on the Odes of Solomon*, vol. 1, *Literary Setting, Textual Studies, Gnosticism, the Dead Sea Scrolls and the Gospel of John* (Sheffield: Sheffield Academic Press, 1998); idem, *The First Christian Hymnbook: The Odes of Solomon* (Eugene, OR: Wipf & Stock, 2009).

9. James D. G. Dunn, *Tertium Genus? A Contested Identity* (Grand Rapids: Eerdmans, 2015); David E. Aune, "The Odes of Solomon and Early Christian Prophecy," *New Testament Studies* 28 (1982): 435–60.

10. Richard Viladesau, *The Beauty of the Cross: The Passion of Christ in Theology and the Arts, from the Catacombs to the Eve of the Renaissance* (Oxford: Oxford University Press, 2006), 42. Also on the *orans*, see Reidar Hvalvik, "Nonverbal Aspects of Early Christian Prayer and the Question of Identity," in *Early Christian Prayer and Identity Formation*, ed. Reidar Hvalvik and Karl Olav Sandnes (Tübingen: Mohr Siebeck, 2014), 82–85. It needs to be noted that at times the difference between upstretched and outstretched hands can be difficult to differentiate.

Syria was also the primary base for Ignatius, the bishop of Antioch. Here we briefly note three places where his references to the cross, the means for "salvation and eternal life" (*Ephesians* 18), include conceptualization of it as a shape of importance. In his letter to Ephesian Christians, he speaks of the cross as holding up and supporting Jesus-followers to keep them from falling away, just as it had supported Jesus (*Ephesians* 9). In his letter to Christians in Smyrna, he speaks of Jesus-followers having been "nailed . . . body and soul to the cross of the Lord Jesus Christ" (*Smyrneans* 1). Elsewhere he likens Jesus-followers to "branches of the cross," a summons for God's people to enjoy unity in Christ (*Trallians* 11). In these ways, the shape of the cross permeated various aspects of Ignatius's thinking, and he seems to assume that this would not be out of place in the thinking of his various audiences.

One final and very important pre-Constantinian text needs to be considered here. *Fifth Ezra* is a Christian text that was probably written in Syria shortly after the Bar Kokhba revolt of 132–135.[12] In 2:23, the risen Lord gives these instructions to his followers: "When you find any [among your walls] who are dead, commit them to the grave and mark it." Those who do this will enjoy "first place in my resurrection."[13] Here the grave of a deceased person is being marked out for protection, by means of a mark whose shape, apparently, everyone was expected to understand. This opens a significant window into Christian conviction in the first half of the second century. The Christian audience of *5 Ezra* was expected

---

11. Paul Corby Finney, "Cross," in *Encyclopedia of Early Christianity*, 2nd ed., ed. Everett Ferguson (New York: Garland, 1997), 304. See also Robin Margaret Jensen, *Understanding Early Christian Art* (New York: Routledge, 2000), 36.

12. See Bruce Longenecker, *2 Esdras* (Sheffield: Sheffield Academic Press, 1995), 114–20, where the date of the text is discussed.

13. One manuscript (C) promises this blessing not to the one who did the marking but to those who have died with this marking added to their graves. See Jacob M. Myers, *I and II Esdras* (Garden City, NY: Doubleday, 1974), 145.

to understand perfectly what is meant by "mark it." There is no description of the shape to be used, and no explanation as to what that shape accomplishes. This is not a theological innovation or idiosyncratic novelty of the author; what he instructs was expected to be readily sensible to his Christian audience—and all this within the second quarter of the second century. In view of the influence of Ezek. 9:4–6 among both Jewish and Christian realia of this period (as already noted), the most obvious candidate for the shape of the mark is the shape of a cross, as noted by Jacob Myers, who suggests that the mark is "a cross sign placed on grave [sic] as a sign of victory."[14] Here, then, eschatological protection and life come to the person who is marked by the cross of Jesus.

What is most important about this text is that it testifies to the fact that the cross was being put to use in ways that went beyond abstract conceptualization and mental visualization already prior to the middle of the second century CE. This text testifies that the cross was not simply an abstract symbol in the realm of theological mind mapping. It also served a role within the concrete realm of physical representation during the imperial reign of either Hadrian or Antonius Pius.[15]

---

14. Ibid., 151.

15. Much the same is suggested by a later text, Eusebius's *Church History*, from the first quarter of the fourth century. In a passage recounting the death of James the brother of Jesus in the year 62, Eusebius states that James's body was buried "on the spot by the temple," claiming that "his monument still remains by the temple" (book 2, chapter 28.18). One Greek manuscript of the work elaborates this claim by adding the following note: "This monument was an unshaped stone, having as an inscription the name of the interred James. From which [example] even until now the Christians set up stones in their tombs, and they either write letters on them, or they cut in the sign of the cross" (reported in Jack Finegan, *The Archaeology of the New Testament: The Life of Jesus and the Beginning of the Early Church* [Princeton, NJ: Princeton University Press, 1992], 356). Existing in a fourth or fifth century manuscript, this note is clearly much later than the mid-second century text of *5 Ezra,* but it imagines that the practice of inscribing the cross on burial plots had existed not only in the author's own day but throughout the centuries. This estimate may require significant historical nuancing, but it illustrates that this post-Constantinian scribe (1) had no conception that the cross had only derived from Constantine's efforts and (2) knew that the inscribed cross was commonly used as a protective identifying mark by Christians.

Just as significant is what the text goes on to say just a few verses later. Speaking of the glory that awaits Christians, the author exhorts them to "Rise and stand, and see at the feast of the Lord the number of those who have been sealed" (2:38). As Michael Knibb has noted, "there appears to be a link with Rev. 7:2–8 [as well as] Rev. 9:4 [and] Ezek. 9:4-6," with these two passages from *5 Ezra* interpreting "the sign" and "seal" as "the sign of the cross."[16] For this author, those who sit at the Lord's table, both in the eschaton and (no doubt) in the present, are those who have been sealed or marked with the sign of the cross, whether that be on their foreheads in life or in their graves at death.

Two other early Christian texts from the late first and early second century have already been dealt with in chapter 2 above—that is, the Johannine Apocalypse and the *Epistle of Barnabas*. At this point, then, with our textual survey complete, we can merge the literary and material data in order to assemble some conclusions about the data's significance.

16. Michael A. Knibb, "Commentary on 2 Esdras," in *The First and Second Books of Esdras*, by R. J. Coggins and M. A. Knibb (Cambridge: Cambridge University Press, 1979), 97 and 95, respectively. See also Myers, *I and II Esdras*, 152, who postulates the same textual linkages.

8

The Cross and Its Advocates

In the preceding chapters it has been demonstrated that (1) the shape of the cross had already made its way into the Christian imagination (in its various permutations) as a theological symbol, and (2) that the cross was visually reproduced as an artistic symbol of Christian devotion long before Constantine ever thought to make it so. This chapter, then, seeks to accomplish several further tasks: it plots the geographical and temporal spread of this symbolic use of the cross; it proposes hypotheses about the potential attraction of the cross in ordinary situations; and it offers a postulate regarding the minimal use of the cross as a symbol per se in the Roman catacombs.

1. The Geographical Spread of the Data

The cross appears as a feature of pre-Constantinian Christian identity in a variety of data whose provenance we can specify. This includes the following geographical areas:

1. Gaza (the bloodstone amulet, with highly syncretistic features);
2. Jerusalem (the jasper gem);
3. Syria (the *Odes of Solomon*; Ignatius; *5 Ezra;* one gemstone; the *Gospel of Thomas*);
4. Alexandria (*Epistle of Barnabas*; Clement; *Books of Jeu*; P46; P66; P75; Origen);
5. northern Africa (Tertullian and Minucius Felix);
6. the Iberian peninsula (signet rings);
7. Asia Minor (Johannine Apocalypse; one signet ring and perhaps others that are not securely locatable; nineteen tombstones; the Eutyches tombstone, if it is a Christian artifact; and perhaps the *Acts of Paul and Thecla*, if it derives from Asia Minor);
8. Rome (Justin Martyr; the catacomb data; the "pagan" mausoleum; the *Aurelii* sepulcher; Hippolytus; Ostian inscriptions); and
9. Pompeii (the cross in the bakery, and perhaps other artifacts not presented here).

There are two things to note about this data. First, in some of these locations, there is a combination of (1) theological discourse about the cross as a Christian sign and (2) indicators that the cross was being used as a concretely formed symbol by Christians—thereby interlocking the two kinds of data in particular regions. So for instance:

- the data from Syria testify to (a) discourse about the cross being a Christian sign and (b) the concrete practice of marking graves with the mark of the cross;

- the data from Alexandria testify to (a) theological discourse about the cross as a symbol of victory and (b) graphic depictions of the cross and of staurographic crucifixions;

- the data from Asia Minor testify to (a) theological discourse about the cross within the signet ring of God and (b) a significant number of tombstones and one or more signet rings; and

- the data from Rome and its environs testify to (a) theological discourse about the sign of the cross and (b) cruciform inscriptions in catacombs, nearby the catacombs, in a sepulcher, and in the Ostian baths.

Of course, these witnesses fall across a century or so, and the geographical region of Asia Minor is sizable. Nonetheless, it is notable that theological discourse about the sign of the cross is found in these four geographical locations and that a physical representation of the cross lies relatively close at hand.

Second, although there are temporal differences among these witnesses, this data nonetheless provides no basis for thinking that the religious symbolism of the cross arose only in localized or anomalous situations among curiously idiosyncratic Christians tucked away in some remote part of the world prior to the fourth century. In fact, some of the geographical regions listed above were prominent centers in the spread of Christianity. It is not surprising, then, that the cross was recognized by Christians and their opponents alike as a symbol of Christian identity—all the more so since Christians frequently communicated with each other across the regions of the Mediterranean basin.[1]

Intercity communication among Christians might even be evident in the texts considered above. Whereas the *Epistle of Barnabas* (somewhere in the eastern Mediterranean in the early second

---

1. For examples of this among Jesus-followers already in the first century, see Michael Thompson, "The Holy Internet: Communication between Churches in the First Christian Generation," in *The Gospels for All Christians: Rethinking the Gospel Audiences*, ed. Richard Bauckham (Grand Rapids: Eerdmans, 1998), 49–70. For second-century examples, compare Ignatius's letters to the churches (for example, *To the Romans* 9.3), or Dionysius of Corinth.

century) recounts Moses's cross-like posture as the key to battle for the Hebrew people, Justin Martyr (in Rome in the mid-second century) picks up this feature and repackages it for his own audience. In this instance, we are probably witnessing a tradition being handed on across the generations in second-century Christianity, with the cross as a Christian symbol being the stable feature in discourses located in distinct geographical regions of the Mediterranean basin.

These observations combine to suggest that, while it is possible that the cross was cherished only by atypical Christianities in the pre-Constantinian period, this possibility looks notably unlikely.

2. The Temporal Spread of the Data

The second thing to take notice of is the temporal spread of the material and literary witnesses. Working backwards from the year 300, we arrive at this reconstruction.

- The Ostian crosses in the Baths of Neptune are pre-Constantinian witnesses, probably from the late third century, or perhaps the early fourth century. The same is true for the late third-century "Christians for Christians" tombstone and some of the other tombstones noted above, together with the Aurelii sepulcher painting from the second half of the third century.

- Signet rings in which the cross features prominently were crafted at some point within the third century, along with the Beratio Nicatora staurogram, Origen's reference to the cross in relation to Ezek. 9:4–6, and Hippolytus's alleged mention of the cross as the mark that seals Christians in faith.

- The first half of the third century includes the following witnesses, most of which fall within the earlier part of that period: the Alexandros tombstone, the Aurelios Satorneinos tombstone, the

166

Artemidoros tombstone, the Deiogas tombstone, the Loukios and Tatia tombstone, the tombstone honoring Asklepiades and Melete, the unnamed tombstone, and the *itchthys* inscription.

- A variety of witnesses bunch up around either the late second or early third centuries. This includes Tertullian, Minucius Felix, Clement of Alexandria, the Rufina catacomb inscription, the "pagan" mausoleum, the original manuscript behind the *Books of Jeu*, the bloodstone amulet, and the staurograms of P66, P75, P46.

- The final two entries in that list (the bloodstone amulet and the staurogram) suggest that the cross was functioning as a symbol of Christian devotion from an even earlier period. Evidence from that earlier period (roughly the second half of the second century) comes from two catacomb inscriptions (the Irene and the triple cross inscriptions), the *Acts of Paul and Thecla,* the Eutyches tombstone, and the jasper gem.

- Justin Martyr stands in the middle of the second century.

- *Fifth Ezra* testifies that in the first half of the second century the cross was being used as a concrete symbol that some Christians tangibly produced within the physical world. This combines easily with the emphasis on the shape of the cross in Ignatius, the *Odes of Solomon,* and the *Epistle of Barnabas.* None of these early second-century witnesses suggest that Christians needed to be educated concerning the pertinence of the cross for Christian identity; instead, they seem simply to assume the point. This is true even of the *Epistle of Barnabas.* Of course, the clever christological symbolism evident in the isopsephic values of *Epistle of Barnabas* 9 may well be attributed to the ingenuity of the author himself, but that does not mean that the religious symbolism of the cross itself derived from his ingenuity. The author provides no instruction

167

about why the cross should be an important symbol for Christians, which might be expected if Christians in his day knew nothing of its symbolic value. Instead, in both chapter 9 and chapter 12 of *Epistle of Barnabas*, there is only ingenuity by means of linking the symbol of the cross to narratives from the Hebrew Bible (one allegedly being a secret tradition) for the benefit of readers—readers who seem not to require any education about the author's pronounced interest in the cross as a central aspect of the Christian story, from which they were to draw their identity.

• The Johannine Apocalypse employs a striking image of the cross as a symbol that lies embedded within the deep affections or identity of the Christian deity. During the last decade of the first century, that text circulated throughout seven major cities of Asia Minor and beyond. Although this might simply be considered a conceptual image struck solely in the mind, the evidence from Pompeii suggests that Jesus-devotion there included eyes that recognized the cross as a potent religious symbol—one that offered benefits and could easily be depicted concretely within a physical, artistic medium.

3. The Shape of the Cross

We can now return to the matter of the way that the cross is formed along the spectrum of these pre-Constantinian witnesses. While the shape of the cross is clear within the material remains, a full taxonomy needs also to include any evidence that can be gleaned from the literary evidence as well. Some of the texts studied in chapter 7 above offer no indication regarding the cruciform shape that they imagine. At times, however, there is some clarity on the matter.

The Johannine Apocalypse is of early relevance. As we have seen, the author drew on the imagery of Ezek. 9:4–6 in Rev. 7:2–3 and, in conformity with a vibrant tradition extending from at least the first century BCE to the third century CE, imagined the cross to be formed as an equilateral cross, (the Paleo-Hebrew letter tav, or "mark"). This formation of the cross lives on in other witnesses too (whether indebted to Ezek. 9:4–6 or not), such as the Rufina and *Iesus* catacomb inscriptions, the gnostic *Books of Jeu*, several signet rings (sometimes in conjunction with other cross shapes), the Eutyches tombstone, the Artemidoros tombstone, the Deiogas tombstone, the Loukios and Tatia tombstone, the Asklepiades and Melete tombstone, the unnamed tombstone, Origen's reference to Ezek. 9:4–6, and the Ostian floor inscriptions.[2]

Another identifiable shape emerges from the *Epistle of Barnabas,* where in chapter 9 the cross is likened to the Greek letter tau, representing a T cross. This formation of the cross also appears in or on the following: the Alexamenos inscription, several signet rings, the Irene catacomb inscription, the gemstone amulet, and various appearances of the staurogram.

The third identifiable shape also emerges from the *Epistle of Barnabas,* where in chapter 12 the cross is conceived of as a body cross, †. This formation reappears in or on the following: a few signet rings, the Aurelii sepulcher painting, most of the tombstone crosses from Asia Minor, Justin Martyr, the *Odes of Solomon,* the *oranic* posture, and a Pompeian bakery (probably in imitation of the Egyptian Ankh of life).

Intriguingly, then, the earliest depictions of the cross do not conform to a single formation. We would be hard-pressed to say that there was an original form from which other forms later derived. We can only recognize that even from the very earliest detectable period, the shape of the cross is variable. (This is no different from,

---

2. The Ostian gamma cross that embeds a staurogram within it can also be mentioned here, since the gamma cross is, in most regards, a variation on the equilateral cross.

say, the depiction of Jesus as the Good Shepherd in early Christian art, where variation is evident.)[3] In fact, sometimes a single artifact or text evidences more than one shape in its depiction of the cross—such as the *Epistle of Barnabas* and several Christian rings. This variety of shapes allowed early Christian theologians scope for exploring the cross's multifaceted potential in terms of its symbolic value.

4. An Apotropaic Function for the Cross?

In the fourth century, Cyril of Jerusalem had this to say about the power of the cross:

> If any disbelieve the power of the Crucified, let him ask the devils; if any believe not words, let him believe what he sees. Many have been crucified throughout the world, but by none of these are the devils scared; but when they see even the Sign of the Cross of Christ, who was crucified for us, they shudder. (*Catechesis*, Lecture 14 [*Patrologia Graeca* 33: 77])

For Cyril, the Christian symbol of the cross channeled apotropaic power, forcing "devils" to shudder and leaving those for whom Christ was crucified free from the malicious influence of the demonic world.

A generation earlier, during the time of the Diocletian persecution (303–311), Lactantius was able to say that though the pagan gods stand behind the oppression of Christians by their contemporaries, since those gods "can neither approach those in whom they shall see the heavenly mark, nor injure those whom the immortal sign as an impregnable wall protects, they harass them by men, and persecute them by the hands of others" (*Divine Institutes* XXVII). The terms "the heavenly mark" and "the immortal sign" can only be references

---

3. See, for instance, Boniface Ramsey, "A Note on the Disappearance of the Good Shepherd from Early Christian Art," *Harvard Theological Review* 76 (1983): 377, where the point is made that patristic literature gives little description of how the Good Shepherd is to be depicted.

to the sign of the cross, which Lactantius imagined as offering protection from invading and malevolent suprahuman forces.[4]

Figure 8.1. A ring (probably Christian from the Byzantine era) with apotropaic defenses against the evil eye imprinted in the shape of a cross.

These texts highlight the protective dimension of the cross. Those who are marked by the cross belong to the almighty deity and are protected from malicious deities and demons.[5]

4. This conforms to what Origen said about the name of Jesus: "The name of Jesus is so powerful against the demons that sometimes it is effective even when pronounced by bad men" (*Against Celsus* 1.6). Compare the six-century phenomenon of tattooing foreheads with the cross as protection against the plague (see Samuel N. C. Lieu and Ken Parry, "Deep into Asia," in *Early Christianity in Contexts: An Exploration across Cultures and Continents*, ed. William Tabbernee [Grand Rapids: Baker Academic, 2014], 152). In the seventh century, a Christian made the sign of the cross in order to dissipate a violent storm brewed up by Turkish shamans (see ibid., 153).

5. In this regard, a most extraordinary passage needs to be referenced here. Although it does not mention the cross as a means of exorcism, we know from our survey in chapter 7 above that Justin Martyr held the cross to be a mark of protection, and perhaps the symbol of the cross was part of the process of exorcism that he describes in *First Apology* 2.6: "He [Jesus] was made man also . . . for the destruction of the demons. And now you can learn this from what is under your own observation. For numberless demoniacs throughout the whole world, and in your city, many of our Christian men exorcising them in the name of Jesus Christ, who was crucified

Something similar is already evident in Rev. 7:2–3 and 9:4, the earliest textual witness to the cross's utility as a Christian symbol. There, the mark that is placed on the foreheads of Jesus-followers offers protection against the invading forces that launch destruction on the created order. Although the suprahuman forces in this instance seem to be operating on behalf of the almighty deity rather than malicious "devils," the protective dimension of the cross derives from the fact that the cross preserves those who are identified by it (drawing on the force of Ezek. 9:4–6).

The same is probably at play in the catacomb crosses, with the cross standing guard (in a sense) over those whose names and bodies appear near it. As we have seen, William Tabbernee suggested much the same function for the cross on the funerary altar of Aurelios Satorneinos (it functioned "as a symbol of protection"). So too, 5 Ezra imagines the mark of the cross to identify the person within the grave, being the sign of the people who celebrate God's eschatological victory. Mentioned by the author of Epistle of Barnabas, by Justin Martyr, and by Cyprian, Moses's outstretched body (replicating the crucifixion of Jesus) serves the function of protecting those who battled opposing forces. Justin also notes that the cross crafted out of bronze by Moses prevented death from coming to the people. Much the same is on display in the beautiful bloodstone amulet, with protection being its key function for the benefit of its owner. The same was likely true for the jasper gem, with its magical function. This corresponds with the testimony of the Testament of Solomon, in which the sign of the cross is said to be the only form of protection against the "lecherous spirit" that seeks to kill its victims or, at the very least, to cause their flesh to be gnawed to

under Pontius Pilate, have healed and do heal, rendering helpless and driving the possessing devils out of the men, though they could not be cured by all the other exorcists, and those who used incantations and drugs."

pieces. And (as I will argue elsewhere in fuller form), an apotropaic function probably motivated the installation of the cross in the bakery of the Insula Arriana Polliana in Pompeii.

Concern for protection against malevolent forces may also have motivated the early Christian practice of marking themselves with the sign of the cross throughout the day. According to Robin Jensen, Tertullian saw this gesture as "an apotropaic sign to ward away evil and to remind Christians daily of their allegiance."[6] Similarly, Thecla is preserved from death on a fiery pyre after having made the sign of the cross (a causal connection being implied). And there might even be a residue of this conviction in the gnostic imagination, where the cross functioned as a means of escape from suprahuman forces that were detrimental to the success of their spiritual journey and that sought to inflict harm on them.

It is, then, easy to imagine the attraction of the cross in a world enmeshed in a thicket of suprahuman influence and manipulation. A variety of Christians seem to have imagined that the cross helped to protect them from suprahuman forces that would threaten them. There is no indication that this protective dimension was a late development. It is embedded within the very earliest traditions surveyed (the Johannine Apocalypse and the *Epistle of Barnabas*) and the earliest Christian artifact (the bakery cross of Pompeii).

It is possible that this apotropaic dimension of the cross already had a foothold in the middle of the first century—some twenty years, perhaps, before the apotropaic cross in Pompeii. Notice, for instance, how in Gal. 3:1 the apostle Paul contrasts "Jesus Christ vividly displayed as crucified before your eyes" with the dangerous situation of being injured by the evil eye (τίς ὑμᾶς ἐβάσκανεν).[7] Some who

---

6. Robin Margaret Jensen, *Understanding Early Christian Art* (New York: Routledge, 2000), 138.
7. For more on this fascinating passage and its relationship to Paul's case in Galatians 4–5, see Bruce Longenecker, "Until Christ Is Formed in You: Suprahuman Forces and Moral Character in Galatians," *Catholic Biblical Quarterly* 61 (1999): 92–108.

heard Paul's message might well have been fascinated by his claim that "the cross is foolishness to those who are perishing, but to us who are being saved it is the power of God" (1 Cor. 1:18). Here the cross is proclaimed as containing the power of an almighty deity, a deity who, according to a different Pauline text, has initiated a "struggle . . . against the cosmic powers of this present darkness, against the spiritual forces of evil in the heavenly places" (Eph. 6:12). We should not be surprised if claims of that kind held formidable attraction for some within the Greco-Roman world, and if on occasion the shape of the cross itself became concretely depicted in order to harness its protective power.

It is, in fact, in this context that the stories of Jesus healing the diseased and expelling malevolent spirits would have been heard among the Greco-Roman populace. These stories were embedded within the message of (some of) the earliest forms of the Jesus-movement, and would have had a ready-made audience among the urban populations of the ancient Mediterranean basin. For instance, Pliny the Elder, who died in the eruption of Mount Vesuvius, tells us that among his contemporaries "there is no one who does not fear to be spellbound" by curses cast against them through suprahuman agents (*Natural History*, 28.4.19). Plutarch tells us that "people with chronic diseases" who have tried all the "ordinary remedies and customary regimes" for healing will "turn to expiations and amulets and dreams" in order to exact a cure (*De facie in orbe lunae* 920B). A second-century papyrus from Oxyrhynchus in Upper Egypt recounts that the deity Asclepius "often saves people after all medical efforts have failed to [liberate them], if only they turn to him in worship, however briefly" (*Oxyrhynchus Papyri* 1381).[8] In this setting, a message about a deity who expunged disease and malevolent spirits

8. D. R. Cartlidge and D. L. Dungan, eds., *Documents for the Study of the Gospels* (London: Collins, 1980), 121–25.

would almost inevitably have had a ready-made audience that was receptive to considering its claims and attractions.[9]

What we are seeing in all this is the potential appeal of Christianity within a culture gripped by fear of suprahuman forces. The point has been well made by Peter Bolt, for instance, in his study of how the Markan Gospel would have resonated with its original Greco-Roman audience. Bolt notes that the healing and exorcism stories in that Gospel "had the potential to make a huge impact upon Graeco-Roman readers, and so to play a large role in the mission, and the remarkable growth, of early Christianity."[10] So too, Dale Martin notes the correlation between the all-pervasive fear of evil in the Greco-Roman world and the rise of the early Jesus-movement:

> Christianity may indeed have been as successful as it was because, among other factors, it offered answers to a problem that most people considered a real one: the threat of harm from possibly malicious daimons. Christianity, unlike classical philosophy, did not answer the problem by insisting that evil daimons did not exist. Instead, it offered an antidote more powerful than the poison, a drug stronger than the disease; healing and exorcism in the name of Jesus.[11]

The fear was real, the anxiety was poignant, and Christianity offered a solution to the problem.

One pervasive fear was the fear of death. Or as one graffito from Pompeii states, "While I live, you, hateful death, are coming" (*CIL*

---

9. See, for instance, Peter G. Bolt, *Jesus' Defeat of Death: Persuading Mark's Early Readers* (Cambridge: Cambridge University Press, 2003); Richard Horsley, *Jesus and Magic: Freeing the Gospel Stories from Modern Misconceptions* (Eugene, OR: Cascade Books, 2014).

10. Bolt, *Jesus' Defeat of Death*, 1.

11. Dale Martin, *Inventing Superstition* (Cambridge, MA: Harvard University Press, 2004), 243. See also Dag Oistein Endsjo, *Greek Resurrection Beliefs and the Success of Christianity* (New York: Palgrave MacMillan, 2009), and P. Gray, *Godly Fear: The Epistle to the Hebrews and Greco-Roman Critiques of Superstition* (Atlanta: Society of Biblical Literature, 2003). Something similar may be evident in the Ἀνάθεμα Ἰησοῦς of 1 Cor. 12:3, if that cryptic phrase is not about cursing Jesus but about cursing one's competitors through the power of Jesus; on this, see Bruce W. Winter, *After Paul Left Corinth: The Influence of Secular Ethics and Social Change* (Grand Rapids: Eerdmans, 2001), 164–83. This interpretation may not be compelling, however.

4.5112; see also figs. 8.1 and 8.2). The fear of death was closely associated with the fear of illness induced by daimons, resulting in people employing magicians to "drag out their life with food drink and magic spells, trying to keep death out of the way" (Euripides, *Suppliants* 1109–11). It does not take much to recognize that, for those in fear of "hateful death," the "good news" of early Christianity might well have had some attraction. Against the backdrop of fear and anxiety, some from the first century might well have wanted to ponder awhile on the claims of those curious Christians who uttered bizarre things like "He who raised Christ from the dead will give life to your mortal bodies" (Rom. 8:11), and "death has been swallowed up in victory" (1 Cor. 15:54). In the ancient world, such audacious claims were neither without rival (compare the popularity of the Isis cult) nor without appeal.

Figure 8.2. From Pompeii I.5.2, a mosaic of Death, the great leveler of rich (left) and poor (right), as the wheel of fortune spins precariously for all life (i.e., even the flap of a butterfly's wing can tilt the balance one way or the other).[12]

12. National Archaeological Museum of Naples, inv. no. 109982; used with permission of the Ministry of Cultural Heritage, Activities and Tourism—Special Superintendency for Archaeological Heritage of Pompeii, Herculaneum and Stabiae, which prohibits the reproduction or duplication of this image.

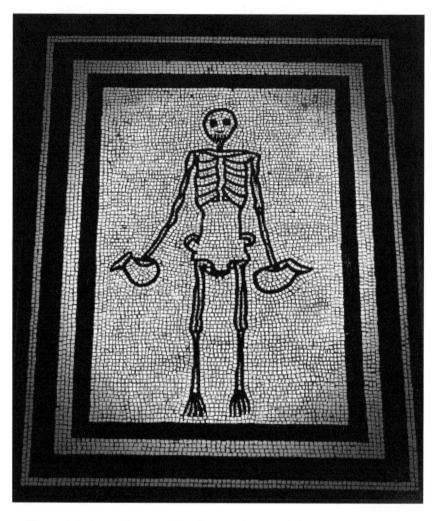

Figure 8.3. A mosaic capturing the cognizance of the ominous fate that awaits one and all (so live life to the fullest in the meantime).[13]

13. National Archaeological Museum of Naples, inv. no. 9978; used with permission of the Ministry of Cultural Heritage, Activities and Tourism—Special Superintendency for Archaeological Heritage of Pompeii, Herculaneum and Stabiae, which prohibits the reproduction or duplication of this image.

5. Why Are There So Few Crosses in Christian Catacombs?

There are several curious anomalies in the material record of the catacombs in Rome. For instance, despite the fact that the anchor was used extensively as a symbol within the earliest second-century Christian catacombs at Rome (e.g., the catacomb of Priscilla), Christian authors of the second and third centuries rarely discuss the symbol or offer a theological interpretation of it. Conversely, although the symbol of the fish is discussed relatively early among Christian authors, it is only in later third-century catacombs that the fish begins to appear as a symbol.[14] So too, although gems with Christian symbols have been discovered throughout the Mediterranean basin of the third century, none with Christian symbols have been found within the catacombs themselves.[15] These three oddities within the catacomb record currently seem to defy explanation.

In light of the evidence from foregoing chapters, a similar oddity involves the relative absence of the cross within the second- and third-century Christian catacombs. Although the cross may be embedded within the many anchors of the early catacombs, it is curious that the cross itself has such a minimal presence there, especially in light of the fact that, for some, the cross was functioning as a Christian symbol during that time.

Perhaps this is just another of those curiosities of the material record. Perhaps indigenous factors were at work that are now beyond

14. These discrepancies have been noted by Emanuele Castelli, "The Symbols of Anchor and Fish in the Most Ancient Parts of the Catacomb of Priscilla: Evidence and Questions," in *Studia Patristica, Vol. LIX: Papers Presented at the Sixteenth International Conference on Patristic Studies Held in Oxford 2011*, ed. Allen Brent and Markus Vinzent (Leuven: Peeters, 2013), 11–19. See also Jeffrey Spier, "The Earliest Christian Art," in *Picturing the Bible: The Earliest Christian Art*, ed. Jeffrey Spier (New Haven, CT: Yale University Press, 2007), 4: "The Christian writers of these years [i.e., late second to early third century] seldom expressed an interest in such images."
15. The point is made by Jeffrey Spier, *Late Antique and Early Christian Gems* (Wiesenbaden: Reichert, 2007), 4.

our historical grasp. On the other hand, data from our survey might go some way toward offering a partial explanation of the oddity.

Particular reference needs to be made to the appearance of cross patterns in the *Books of Jeu* that derive from a second- or early third-century original, and to the appearance of the cross in a painting within the Aurelii sepulcher in the last quarter of the third century. Another artifact, the jasper gem mentioned in chapter 5, has also been identified as gnostic. These are suggestive that some gnostic Christians from second and third centuries were using the symbol of the cross as a means of escaping from the deity who had created the world. (Compare also the appearance of the staurogram within saying 55 of the fourth-century Coptic manuscript of the *Gospel of Thomas* [Nag Hammadi, codex II, tractate 2].)

The literary record shares the same testimony. Around the year 180, the proto-orthodox theologian Irenaeus claimed that gnostic "heretics" were guilty of "perverse interpretations and deceitful expositions" (*Against Heresies* 1.3.6). Among his many charges, he accuses them of hijacking what they call "Stauros" (i.e., "the cross"), devaluing it so that it means little other than the divine "sustaining power," a power that burns up the whole of the material realm (1.3.5). This, they say, is what Jesus meant when he said, "Take up the cross and follow me" (cf. Mark 8:34 and parallels); further, they claim it is what Paul meant when he said, "The doctrine of the cross is to them that perish foolishness, but to us who are saved it is the power of God" (1 Cor. 1:18), or when he said, "God forbid that I should glory in anything except in the cross of Christ, by whom the world is crucified to me, and I to the world" (Gal. 6:14). Interestingly, this is precisely the combination of sayings from Jesus and Paul reflected in the *Books of Jeu*, as noted in chapter 5 above.

We have, then, good corroborating evidence demonstrating that some gnostic Christians were conscripting the cross and filling it with fresh significance, so that "Stauros" became for them the divine power that will consume the created order by fire. This interpretation was pressed beyond theological conceptualization and incorporated into concrete symbolism, as testified to by the crosses found in the *Books of Jeu,* the Aurelii sepulcher, and (later) by the Nag Hammadi Coptic manuscript of the *Gospel of Thomas.*

With this as a backdrop, it is not difficult to imagine that some proto-orthodox Christians might well have become wary of using the cross as a symbol in tomb environments. Because the cross had already been adopted in some gnostic circles as a means of escape from the created order by ascending to a deity far superior to (and in conflict with) the deity of creation, perhaps proto-orthodox devotees of Jesus based in Rome felt there was a disincentive to feature the cross as a form of symbolic self-identification in the environment of their grave sites. Perhaps they imagined that using a cross in that context might send signals that would potentially jeopardize their prospects for resurrection by the creator deity. If the sign of the cross served a protective function in the everyday lives of proto-orthodox Christians, its adoption as a protective device by gnostic Christians seeking to avoid the creator deity may have rendered the cross an inappropriate symbol for inclusion on the tombs of those who wanted eschatological protection from that very deity. The same cross that functioned as an unambiguous religious symbol within the daily lives of many Christians (perhaps with primarily a protective function) may have been open to misinterpretation in the context of the tombs of the dead, since the cross had become an instrument of gnostic transmigration after death. As a consequence of that development, proto-orthodox Christians in Rome may have estimated that marking a tomb with a cross might have sailed too close to the wind, risking the prospects of their eternal salvation.

This simple explanation may also illustrate why Christian crosses from the third century usually appear alongside accompanying symbols firmly established within proto-orthodox circles of Christianity. Those accompanying symbols (e.g., the fish, the chi of Χριστός) lent interpretative clarity to the symbolic value of the cross itself. So, for instance, the third-century signet rings found in Christian graves on the Iberian peninsula depict the cross and the fish together—with the cross serving as an eschatological mark of identity coupled with a symbol that was clearly associated with proto-orthodox forms of Christianity.[16] The same is true for the Christian cross found on the "pagan" mausoleum, where it is accompanied by the *ichthys* acrostic. It is also true of some rings in which the cross is featured with the words "Jesus" or "savior," or the letter chi. Only when the cross became so predominantly featured in Constantinian Christianity over and above its less-impressive presence in gnostic Christianity could earlier proto-orthodox concerns about adopting an otherwise ambiguous symbol fall by the wayside, with the cross freed from the need to associate it with other Christian symbols as a consequence.

Moreover, the evidence from *5 Ezra* fits well within this hypothesis. Written around 140 or so, *5 Ezra* is able to imagine what the later catacombs in Rome show sparse evidence of—the protective sign of the cross solely adorning Christian graves. This fits well within the timeline being proposed here. When some "gnostic" Christians in the second half of the second century began adopting the sign of the cross as a form of escaping from the creator deity, the practice of marking graves with the sign of the cross seems to have become vulnerable to eschatological misinterpretation; prior to

16. Compare the following comment in Julia Valeva and Athanosios K. Vionis, "The Balkan Peninsula," in *Early Christianity in Contexts*, 354: "Most Thracian early Christian tombs were, however, decorated with crosses and monograms of Christ—secure protective signs. Very often the letters alpha and omega reinforced the eschatological meaning of the symbols."

that period, however, some Christians marked the graves of others solely with the sign of the cross in order to identify them as worthy of eschatological salvation. Although the practice of marking grave sites with the sign of the cross lived on for some (as testified to by the "Christians for Christians" inscription), others (such as proto-orthodox Christians in Rome) seem to have developed an aversion to that practice, possibly since the symbol of the cross had been co-opted by gnostic Christians in a fashion that problematized its use at proto-orthodox grave sites.

Although this hypothesis can never be held with tenacity, it might well be that the adoption of the cross by some gnosticizing Christians in the second half of the second century transformed the trajectory of the material record enormously, evidenced in the contrast between 5 *Ezra* and the catacombs of Rome regarding the presence of the cross at grave sites.

9

A Very Short Conclusion

Rather than imagining that the cross did not function as a Christian symbol prior to the time of Constantine, we have seen that the cross was, in fact, an important theological symbol among many pre-Constantinian Christians. The spread of imperial Christianity in the fourth century and beyond was not branded under a formerly unused symbol; instead, the melding together of diverse groups into a united empire included the harnessing of a symbol that already had some currency across various Christianities prior to Constantine.

If that is the main thesis of this book, I need also to be clear about what is not being asserted. First, it is not possible to claim that the cross was *the* primary sign of Jesus-devotion across the board in the emerging Christianities of the first three centuries. We have seen that the sign was widespread and well known in certain Christian circles prior to the fourth century, and we have seen that many of those circles were prominently positioned as axis points in the spread of pre-Constantinian Christianities. Nonetheless, it cannot simply be assumed that the cross was appreciated for its religious significance in all sectors of early Christianity throughout the Mediterranean basin. Widespread does not necessarily mean ubiquitous. For instance, for those Christians whose faith tended toward exclusivist devotion and who found themselves living in contexts where the threat of persecution was high, advertising their faith in any fashion would obviously have raised the level of danger against them. Even if they had known of other Jesus-followers with a different religious posture or in a different context who were adopting the cross as a religious symbol, they might well have been averse to adopting it for themselves.

Second, it is not being asserted that the cross had the prominence in pre-Constantinian Christianities that it had in the fourth century and beyond. The cross increasingly rose to a position of particular prominence within and beyond the Constantinian era. As Keith Hopkins rightly notes, "The church's greatest advance during the fourth century lay in the field of symbolic self-advertisement. . . . Its symbolic growth was achieved . . . by the pervasive penetration of Christian symbolism into the visual and private worlds of believers."[1] The cross played a central role in the growth of the symbolic self-advertisement of a religion "that had been meeting in humble structures" but suddenly found itself "housed in magnificent public buildings."[2]

Third, it is not being asserted that crosses were central features in the architecture of Christian worship prior to Constantine. The evidence for the architectural use of the cross in Christian worship in pre-Constantinian contexts is not at hand.[3]

1. Keith Hopkins, *A World Full of Gods: The Strange Triumph of Christianity* (New York: The Free Press, 2000), 130.
2. Rodney Stark, *For the Glory of God: How Monotheism Led to Reformations, Science, Witch-Hunts, and the End of Slavery* (Princeton, NJ: Princeton University Press, 2003), 34.
3. See Vasilios Tzaferis, "Early Christian Churches at Magen," in *Ancient Churches Revealed*, ed. Yoram Tsafrir (Jerusalem: Israel Exploration Society, 1993), 283–85, for a fourth-century church that embeds the cross within its floor pattern.

Fourth, it is not being asserted that these instances of crosses within the material record were all attempts to advertise the Christian faith or to display Christian advocacy to the non-Christian world. Some may have that kind of character (for instance, the rings shown in fig. 5.11), but others might be interpreted as much more guarded and reserved in their function (for instance, the inscriptions in the Ostian Baths of Neptune). It might be interesting to devise a taxonomic scale from guardedness to openness and to propose how relevant artifacts might be placed along that scale. A broad spectrum of this kind is precisely the sort of thing that has been missing from discussions of the cross in the pre-Constantinian world, and as a consequence, one end of the spectrum has been allowed to dictate the terms of engagement and to rule out certain possibilities that, as we have seen, should never have been ruled out.

What is it, then, that we have seen? What is most striking, perhaps, is how a preponderance of the evidence lines up along a certain axis regarding the function of the symbolic cross. In some Christianities prior to Constantine, the cross was regarded first and foremost as a means to mark people out as possessions of the almighty deity.[4] There may have been more to it than that, but there was rarely less than that.

This is the context out of which the cross's notable apotropaic function emerges. This symbol sent the message to suprahuman entities that to mess with people associated with the cross is to mess with a supreme power—a power that even the forces of death cannot conquer. Prior to Constantine, the cross was not primarily an aid to Christian worship or a feature of Christian architecture adorning centralized places of collective adoration; instead, it was often used as an all-important mark of identity in an insecure world in which evil lurked virtually everywhere. It shielded its beneficiaries in a

---

4. This was true not only for some proto-orthodox forms of Christianity but also for some gnostic Christianities, although in a different theological system.

world threatened by the constant insurgency of evil. It offered the protection of the deity who underwent death's defeat but who rose to a victorious life over the most feared of all enemies.

Evidently, then, the cross was about divine power all along. It did not take Constantine to figure that out. His main "contribution" in this area was in harnessing the symbol of the cross to a political agenda.[5] (And if he was the first to do this, he was certainly not the last.) If the cross served an important role in the unification of a diverse empire in the fourth century and beyond, this was partially due to the fact that it had already been recognized as a symbol of power by many Christians who lived in this dangerous world even prior to Constantine.

5. Compare Julia Valeva and Athanosios K. Vionis, "The Balkan Peninsula," in *Early Christianity in Contexts: An Exploration across Cultures and Continents*, ed. William Tabbernee (Grand Rapids: Baker Academic, 2014), 368: "Official imperial imagery was inconceivable without the victorious Christian symbol: the cross."

Bibliography

Adams, Edward. *The Earliest Christian Meeting Places: Almost Exclusively Houses?* New York: Bloomsbury T & T Clark, 2013.

Aland, Barbara, Kurt Aland, Johannes Karavidopoulos, Carlo M. Martini, and Bruce M. Metzger. *Novum Testamentum Graece (New Testament in Greek) (NA28-T).* Nestle-Aland, 28th rev. ed. Institut für Neutestamentliche Textforschung Münster/Westfalen. Stuttgart: Deutsche Bibelgesellschaft, 2012.

Aland, Kurt. "Bemerkungen zum Alter und Entstehung des Christogramms anhand von Beobachtungen bei P66 und P75." In *Studien zur Überlieferung des Neuen Testaments und seines Textes*, 173–79. Berlin: de Gruyter, 1967.

Alexander, Patrick, John F. Kutsko, James D. Ernest, Shirley Decker-Lucke, and David L. Petersen, eds. *The SBL Handbook of Style for Ancient Near Eastern, Biblical, and Early Christian Studies.* Peabody, MA: Hendrickson, 1999.

Aune, David E. "The Odes of Solomon and Early Christian Prophecy." *New Testament Studies* 28 (1982): 435–60.

———. *Revelation 6-16.* Word Biblical Commentary 52b. Nashville: Thomas Nelson, 1998.

Bagnall, Roger. *Everyday Writing in the Greco-Roman East.* Berkeley: University of California Press, 2011.

Balch, David L. "Paul's Portrait of Christ Crucified (Gal. 3:1) in Light of Paintings and Sculptures of Suffering and Death in Pompeian and Roman Houses." In *Early Christian Families in Context: An Interdisciplinary Dialogue*, ed. David L. Balch and Carolyn Osiek, 84–108. Grand Rapids: Eerdmans, 2003.

———. "Rich Pompeian Houses, Shops for Rent, and the Huge Apartment Building as Typical Spaces for Pauline House Churches." *Journal for the Study of the New Testament* 27 (2004): 27–46.

———. "The Suffering of Isis/Io and Paul's Portrait of Christ Crucified (Gal. 3:1): Frescoes in Pompeian and Roman Houses and in the Temple of Isis in Pompeii." *The Journal of Religion* 83 (2003): 24–55.

Baldi, Agnello. *La Pompei: Giudaico-Cristiana*. Cava de Tirreni: Di Mauro Editore, 1964.

Bauckham, Richard. *The Climax of Prophecy: Studies on the Book of Revelation*. Edinburgh: T & T Clark, 1993.

———. *Jesus and the God of Israel: God Crucified and Other Studies on the New Testament's Christology of Divine Identity*. Grand Rapids: Eerdmans, 2008.

Bauer, Walter. *Rechtgläubigkeit und Ketzerei im ältesten Christentum*. Tübingen: J. C. B. Mohr, 1934. Translated as *Orthodoxy and Heresy in Earliest Christianity*. Translated by Robert Kraft. Philadelphia: Fortress Press, 1971.

Beale, G. K. *The Book of Revelation: A Commentary on the Greek Text*. Grand Rapids: Eerdmans, 1999.

Becatti, G. *Scavi di Ostia, IV: Mosaici e Pavimenti Marmorei, Vols. I & II*. Rome: Libreria della Stato, 1961.

Benson, George Willard. *The Cross: Its History and Symbolism. An Account of the Symbol More Universal in Its Use and More Important in Its Significance Than Any Other in the World*. Buffalo: George Willard Benson, 1934.

Bolt, Peter G. *Jesus' Defeat of Death: Persuading Mark's Early Readers*. Cambridge: Cambridge University Press, 2003.

Borg, Marcus J., and John Dominic Crossan. *The First Paul: Reclaiming the Radical Vision behind the Church's Conservative Icon.* London: SPCK, 2009.

Boring, M. Eugene. *Revelation.* Louisville: Westminster John Knox, 1989.

Boyarin, Daniel. *The Jewish Gospels: The Story of the Jewish Christ.* New York: The New Press, 2011.

Bragantini, Irene. "The Cult of Isis and Ancient Egyptomania in Campania." In *Contested Spaces: Houses and Temples in Roman Antiquity and the New Testament,* ed. David L. Balch and Annette Weissenrieder, 21–34. Tübingen: Mohr Siebeck, 2012.

Brakker, David. *The Gnostics: Myth, Ritual, and Diversity in Early Christianity.* Cambridge, MA: Harvard University Press, 2010.

Breeze, David J. *Hadrian's Wall.* 2nd ed. London: English Heritage, 2003.

Bremmer, Jan Nicolaas. "*Christianus sum*: The Early Christian Martyrs and Christ." In *Eulogia: Mélanges offerts à Antoon A.R. Bastiaensen,* ed. G. J. M. Bartelink, A. Hilhorst, and C. H. Kneepkens, 11–20. The Hague: Nijhoff International, 1991.

Brilliant, Richard. *Pompeii: AD 79: The Treasure of Rediscovery.* New York: Clarkson N. Potter, 1979.

Brookins, Timothy A. *Corinthian Wisdom, Stoic Philosophy, and the Ancient Economy.* Cambridge: Cambridge University Press, 2014.

Butterworth, G. W. *Clement of Alexandria.* Loeb 92. New York: G. P. Putnam's Sons, 1919.

Calder, William M. "Early-Christian Epitaphs from Phrygia." *Anatolian Studies* 5 (1955): 25–38.

———. "Philadelphia and Montanism." *Bulletin of the John Rylands Library* 7 (1922–23): 309–52.

Carey, Greg. *Sinners: Jesus and His Earliest Followers.* Waco, TX: Baylor University Press, 2009.

Carter, Warren. "Review of John Granger Cook, *Roman Attitudes Toward the Christians: From Claudius to Hadrian.* Tübingen: Mohr Siebeck: 2010."

Review of Biblical Literature (June 2014). http://www.bookreviews.org/pdf/8676_9535.pdf.

Cartlidge, D. R., and D. L. Dungan, eds. *Documents for the Study of the Gospels.* London: Collins, 1980.

Castelli, Emanuele. "The Symbols of Anchor and Fish in the Most Ancient Parts of the Catacomb of Priscilla: Evidence and Questions." In *Studia Patristica, Vol. LIX: Papers Presented at the Sixteenth International Conference on Patristic Studies Held in Oxford 2011*, ed. Allen Brent and Markus Vinzent, 11–19. Leuven: Peeters, 2013.

Chapman, David W. *Ancient Jewish and Christian Perceptions of Crucifixion.* Grand Rapids: Baker Academic, 2008.

Charlesworth, James H. *Critical Reflections on the Odes of Solomon.* Vol. 1, *Literary Setting, Textual Studies, Gnosticism, the Dead Sea Scrolls and the Gospel of John.* Sheffield: Sheffield Academic Press, 1998.

———. *The First Christian Hymnbook: The Odes of Solomon.* Eugene, OR: Wipf & Stock, 2009.

———. *The Old Testament Pseudepigrapha.* Vol. 2. Garden City, NY: Doubleday, 1985.

Chester, Andrew. "High Christology—When, When, and Why?" *Early Christianity* 2 (2011): 22–50.

Comfort, Philip W., and David P. Barnett. *The Text of the Earliest New Testament Manuscripts.* Wheaton, IL: Tyndale House, 1999.

Cook, John Granger. *Crucifixion in the Mediterranean World.* Tübingen: Mohr Siebeck, 2014.

———. "Review of Gunnar Samuelsson's *Crucifixion in Antiquity: An Inquiry into the Background and Significance of the New Testament Terminology of Crucifixion.*" *Review of Biblical Literature* (April 2014).

———. "Roman Crucifixions: From the Second Punic War to Constantine." *Zeitschrift für neutestamentliche Wissenschaft* 104 (2013): 1–32.

Crossan, John Dominic. *The Cross That Spoke: The Origins of the Passion Narrative.* San Francisco: HarperCollins, 1992.

——. *The Historical Jesus: The Life of a Jewish Mediterranean Peasant.* San Francisco: HarperCollins, 1991.

Croy, N. Clayton. "Review of Candida R. Moss, *The Myth of Persecution.*" *Review of Biblical Literature* (October 2013).

Cumont, Franz. *Textes et monuments figurés relatifs aux mystères de Mithra, publiés avec une introduction critique.* Vol. 2. Brussels: H. Lamertin, 1896.

Curtis, Robert I. "The Garum Debate: Was There a Kosher Roman Delicacy at Pompeii?" *Biblical Archaeological Society: Bible History Daily* (blog). January 25, 2012. http://www.biblicalarchaeology.org/daily/archaeology-today/biblical-archaeology-topics/the-garum-debate/.

Davis, B. S. "The Meaning of *Proegraphē* in the Context of Galatians 3:1." *New Testament Studies* 45 (1999): 194–212.

Derchain, Philippe. "Die älteste Darstellung des Gekreuzigten auf einer magischen Gemme des 3. (?) Jahrhunderts." In *Christentum am Nil,* ed. K. Wessel, 109–13. Recklinghausen: Bongers, 1964.

di Segni, Leah. "Engraved Gem with Greek Magic(?) Inscription, Late Roman (?)." In *Corpus Inscriptionum Iudaeae/Palaestinae,* vol. 1.2, *Jerusalem, Part 2: 705-1120,* ed. Hannah M. Cotton, Leah di Segni, Werner Eck, Benjamine Isaac, Alla Kushnir-Stein, Haggai Misgav, Jonathan J. Price, and Ada Yardeni, 69. Berlin: de Gruyter, 2012.

Di Stephano Manzella, I. *Le iscrizioni dei cristiani in Vaticano: Materiali e contributi scientifici per una mostra epigrafica.* Vatican City: Edizioni Quasar, 1997.

Dinkler, Erich. "Comments on the History of the Symbol of the Cross." *Journal for Theology and the Church* 1 (1965): 124–46. Originally published as "Zur Geschichte des Kreuzsymbols." *Zeitschrift für Theologie und Kirche* 48 (1951): 148–72.

———. "Kreuzzeichen und Kreuz." *Jahrbuch für Antike und Christentum* 5 (1962): 93–112.

———. *Signum Crucis.* Tübingen: Mohr Siebeck, 1967.

Drijvers, Jan W. *Helena Augusta: The Mother of Constantine the Great and the Legend of Her Finding of the True Cross.* Leiden: Brill, 1992.

Dunn, James D. G. *Tertium Genus? A Contested Identity.* Grand Rapids: Eerdmans, 2015.

Dyer, Thomas H. *Pompeii: Its History, Buildings and Antiquities.* London: George Bell & Sons, 1875 [1868].

Ehrman, Bart D. *Lost Christianities.* New York: Oxford University Press, 2003.

Endsjo, Dag Oistein. *Greek Resurrection Beliefs and the Success of Christianity.* New York: Palgrave MacMillan, 2009.

Englemann, Josef. "Glyptic." *Reallexikon für Antike und Christentum* 11 (1981): 270–313.

Evans, Craig A. *Jesus and the Ossuaries: What Jewish Burial Practices Reveal about the Beginning of Christianity.* Waco, TX: Baylor University Press, 2003.

Feldmeier, Reinhard. *The First Letter of Peter.* Waco, TX: Baylor University Press, 2008.

Ferguson, Everett. *Backgrounds of Early Christianity.* 3rd ed. Grand Rapids: Eerdmans, 2003.

———. *Baptism in the Early Church: History, Theology, and Liturgy in the First Five Centuries.* Grand Rapids: Eerdmans, 2009.

———. *Church History.* Grand Rapids: Zondervan, 2005.

Finegan, Jack. *The Archaeology of the New Testament: The Life of Jesus and the Beginning of the Early Church.* Princeton, NJ: Princeton University Press, 1992 [orig. 1969].

Finney, Paul Corby. "Cross." In *Encyclopedia of Early Christianity*, 2nd ed., ed. Everett Ferguson, 303–5. New York: Garland, 1997.

Gardner Coates, Victoria C. "Théodore Chassériau." In *The Last Days of Pompeii: Decadence, Apocalypse, Resurrection*, ed. Victoria C. Gardner Coates, Kenneth Lapatin, and Jon L. Seydl, 100–102. Los Angeles: The J. Paul Getty Museum, 2012.

Gesenius, Wilhelm. *Gesenius' Hebrew Grammar*. Translated by A. E. Cowley. Edited by E. Kautzsch. Oxford: Clarendon, 1910.

Giordano, Carlo, and Isidoro Kahn. *The Jews in Pompeii, Herculaneum, Stabiae and in the Cities of Campania Felix*. 3rd ed. Trans. Wilhelmina F. Jashemski. Rome: Bardi Editore, 2001.

Gray, P. *Godly Fear: The Epistle to the Hebrews and Greco-Roman Critiques of Superstition*. Atlanta: Society of Biblical Literature, 2003.

Green, Joel B. "Identity and Engagement in a Diverse World: Pluralism and Holiness in 1 Peter." *Asbury Theological Journal* 55 (2010): 85–92.

Grig, Lucy. *Making Martyrs in Late Antiquity*. London: Duckworth, 2004.

Grossberg, A. "Behold, The Temple: Is it Depicted on a Priestly Ossuary?" *Biblical Archaeology Review* 22, no. 3 (1996): 46–51, 66.

Guarducci, Margherita. *Epigraphia Greca*. Volume 4. Rome: 1978.

Haas, Christopher. "The Caucasus." In *Early Christianity in Contexts: An Exploration across Cultures and Continents*, ed. William Tabbernee, 111–43. Grand Rapids: Baker Academic, 2014.

Hachlili, Rachael. "Ancient Jewish Burial." In *The Anchor Bible Dictionary*, ed. David Noel Freedman, 1:789–94. New York: Doubleday, 1992.

Harley, Felicity, and Jeffrey Spier. "Magical Amulet with the Crucifixion." In *Picturing the Bible: The Earliest Christian Art*, ed. Jeffrey Spier, 228–29. New Haven, CT: Yale University Press, 2007.

Harley-McGowan, Felicity. "The Constanza Carnelian and the Development of Crucifixion Iconography in Late Antiquity." In *"Gems of Heaven": Recent Research on Engraved Gemstones in Late Antiquity c. AD 200–600*, ed. Chris Entwistle and Noël Adams, 214–20. London: The British Museum Press, 2011.

———. "Engraved Gem with the Crucifixion." In *Picturing the Bible: The Earliest Christian Art*, ed. Jeffrey Spier, 228–29. New Haven, CT: Yale University Press, 2007.

Hays, Richard B. *The Moral Vision of the New Testament: A Contemporary Introduction to New Testament Ethics.* San Francisco: HarperOne, 1996.

Heim, S. Mark. "Missing the Cross? Types of the Passion in Early Christian Art." *Contagion: Journal of Violence, Mimesis, and Culture* 11–12 (2006): 183–94.

Hengel, Martin. *Crucifixion.* Minneapolis: Fortress Press, 1977.

Hengel, Martin, and Anna Maria Schwemer. *Paul between Damascus and Antioch.* London: SCM Press, 1997.

Hislop, Alexander. *The Two Babylons, or The Papal Worship Proved to be the Worship of Nimrod and His Wife.* Neptune, NJ: Loizeaux Brothers, 1916.

Hopkins, Keith. *A World Full of Gods: The Strange Triumph of Christianity.* New York: The Free Press, 2000.

Horbury, William. "Jewish-Christian Relations in Barnabas and Justin Martyr." In *Jews and Christians: The Parting of the Ways, A.D. 70–135*, ed. J. D. G. Dunn, 315–46. Tübingen: Mohr Siebeck, 1992.

Horn, Cornelia, Samuel N. C. Lieu, and Robert R. Phenix Jr. "Beyond the Eastern Frontier." In *Early Christianity in Contexts: An Exploration across Cultures and Continents*, ed. William Tabbernee, 63–110. Grand Rapids: Baker Academic, 2014.

Horrell, David G. "Domestic Space and Christian Meetings at Corinth: Imagining New Contexts and the Building East of the Theatre." *New Testament Studies* 50 (2004): 349–69.

———. "The Label Χριστιανός: 1 Peter 4:16 and the Formation of Christian Identity." *Journal of Biblical Literature* 126 (2007): 361–81.

Horsley, Richard. *Jesus and Magic: Freeing the Gospel Stories from Modern Misconceptions.* Eugene, OR: Cascade Books, 2014.

Hurtado, Larry W. "The Earliest Evidence of an Emerging Christian Material and Visual Culture: The Codex, the Nomina Sacra and the Staurogram." In *Text and Artifact in the Religions of Mediterranean Antiquity: Essays in Honour of Peter Richardson*, ed. Stephen G. Wilson and Michel Desjardins, 271–88. Waterloo, ON: Wilfrid Laurier University Press, 2000.

———. *Lord Jesus Christ: Devotion to Jesus in Earliest Christianity.* Grand Rapids: Eerdmans, 2005.

———. *One God, One Lord: Early Christian Devotion and Ancient Jewish Monotheism.* Minneapolis: Fortress Press, 1988.

———. "The Staurogram." In *The Earliest Christian Artifacts: Manuscripts and Christian Origins*, 135–54. Grand Rapids: Eerdmans, 2006.

———. "The Staurogram: Earliest Depiction of Jesus' Crucifixion." *Biblical Archaeology Review* 39 (2013).

———. "The Staurogram in Early Christian Manuscripts: The Earliest Visual Reference to the Crucified Jesus?" In *New Testament Manuscripts: Their Texts and Their World*, ed. T. J. Kraus and T. Nicklas, 207–26. Boston: Brill, 2006.

Hvalvik, Reidar. "Nonverbal Aspects of Early Christian Prayer and the Question of Identity." In *Early Christian Prayer and Identity Formation*, ed. Reidar Hvalvik and Karl Olav Sandnes, 57–90. Tübingen: Mohr Siebeck, 2014.

Iverson, Kelly. "The Centurion's Confession: A Performance-Critical Analysis of Mark 15:39." *Journal of Biblical Literature* 130 (2011): 329–50.

Jensen, Robin Margaret. *Understanding Early Christian Art.* New York: Routledge, 2000.

Jensen, Robin M., Peter Lampe, William Tabbernee, and D. H. Williams. "Italy and Environs." In *Early Christianity in Contexts: An Exploration across Cultures and Continents*, ed. William Tabbernee, 379–432. Grand Rapids: Baker Academic, 2014.

Jewett, Robert. *Romans: A Commentary*. Minneapolis: Fortress Press, 2006.

Johnson, William. "The Ancient Book." In *The Oxford Handbook of Papyrology*, ed. R. S. Bagnall, 257–81. Oxford: Oxford University Press, 2009.

Keith, Chris, and Tom Thatcher. "The Scar of the Cross: The Violence Ratio and the Earliest Christian Memories of Jesus." In *Jesus, the Voice, and the Text: Beyond The Oral and the Written Gospel*, ed. Tom Thatcher, 197–214. Waco, TX: Baylor University Press, 2008.

Kennedy, C. A. "Early Christians and the Anchor." *Biblical Archaeologist* 38 (1975): 115–24.

King, Karen L. *What Is Gnosticism?* Cambridge, MA: Belknap, 2003.

Knibb, Michael A. "Commentary on 2 Esdras." In *The First and Second Books of Esdras*, by R. J. Coggins and M. A. Knibb, 76–307. Cambridge: Cambridge University Press, 1979.

Kraft, Robert A. *Barnabas and the Didache*. New York: Nelson, 1965.

Krodel, Gerhard A. *Revelation*. Minneapolis: Augsburg Fortress, 1989.

Lampe, Peter. *From Paul to Valentinius: Christians at Rome in the First Two Centuries*. Minneapolis: Fortress, 2003. German original, *Stadtrömischen Christen in den ersten beiden Jahrhunderten*. Tübingen: Mohr Siebeck, 1987.

Liebeschuetz, J. H. W. G. *Continuity and Change in Roman Religion*. Oxford: Oxford University Press, 1996.

Lieu, Samuel N. C., and Ken Parry. "Deep into Asia." In *Early Christianity in Contexts: An Exploration across Cultures and Continents*, ed. William Tabbernee, 143–80. Grand Rapids: Baker Academic, 2014.

Litfin, Bryan M. *Early Christian Martyr Stories. An Evangelical Introduction with New Translations*. Grand Rapids: Baker Academic, 2014.

Litwa, M. David. *Iesus Deus: The Early Christian Depiction of Jesus as a Mediterranean God*. Minneapolis: Fortress Press, 2014.

Longenecker, Bruce. *Hitler, Jesus, and Our Common Humanity: A Jewish Survivor Interprets Life, History, and the Gospels.* Eugene, OR: Cascade, 2014.

———. *Remember the Poor: Paul, Poverty, and the Greco-Roman World.* Grand Rapids: Eerdmans, 2010.

———. *2 Esdras.* Sheffield: Sheffield Academic Press, 1995.

———. "Until Christ Is Formed in You: Suprahuman Forces and Moral Character in Galatians." *Catholic Biblical Quarterly* 61 (1999): 92–108.

———. *The Crosses of Pompeii: Jesus-Devotion in the Shadow of Vesuvius.* Minneapolis: Fortress Press, 2016.

Longenecker, Bruce, and Todd Still. *Thinking through Paul: A Survey of His Life, Letters, and Theology.* Grand Rapids: Zondervan, 2014.

MacDonald, Lee Martin. "The Burial of Jesus, Jewish Burial Practices, and Roman Crucifixion." In *The Tomb of Jesus and His Family? Exploring Ancient Jewish Tombs near Jerusalem's Walls*, ed. James H. Charlesworth, 247–76. Grand Rapids: Eerdmans, 2013.

Marcus, Joel. "Crucifixion as Parodic Exaltation." *Journal of Biblical Literature* 125 (2006): 73–87.

Martin, Dale. *Inventing Superstition.* Cambridge, MA: Harvard University Press, 2004.

Mazois, François. *Les Ruines de Pompeii.* 4 vols. Paris: F. Didot, 1824.

McCane, Byron R. *Roll Back the Stone: Death and Burial in the World of Jesus.* Harrisburg, PA: Trinity Press International, 2003.

Meeks, Wayne A. *The Origins of Christian Morality: The First Two Centuries.* New Haven, CT: Yale University Press, 1995.

Meggitt, Justin J. "Artemidorus and the Johannine Crucifixion." *Journal of Higher Criticism* 5 (1998): 203–8.

———. "Laughing and Dreaming at the Foot of the Cross: Context and Reception of a Religious Symbol." In *Modern Spiritualities: An Inquiry*, ed. Laurence Brown, Bernard C. Farr, and R. Joseph Hoffmann, 9–14. Oxford: Prometheus Books, 1997.

Meijer, Wim G. "If It Walks Like a Duck: Ossuary 6 of the Talpiot 'Patio' Tomb Depicts Commonly Used Jewish Symbols." On *NT Blog*, Mark Goodacre. November 19, 2013. http://ntweblog.blogspot.com/2013/11/if-it-walks-like-duck-ossuary-6-of.html.

Merdinger, Jane. "Roman North Africa." In *Early Christianity in Contexts: An Exploration across Cultures and Continents*, ed. William Tabbernee, 223–60. Grand Rapids: Baker Academic, 2014.

Meyers, Eric M., and Mark A. Chauncey. *Alexander to Constantine: Archaeology of the Land of the Bible, Volume III.3.* New Haven, CT: Yale University Press, 2012.

Mitchell, Stephen. *Anatolia: Land, Men, and Gods in Asia Minor.* 2 vols. Oxford: Clarendon, 1993.

Monnier, Marc. *The Wonders of Pompeii.* Translation. New York: Scribner, 1870.

Moss, Candida R. *Ancient Christian Martyrdom: Diverse Practices, Theologies, and Traditions.* New Haven, CT: Yale University Press, 2012.

———. *The Myth of Persecution: How Early Christians Invented a Story of Martyrdom.* New York: HarperOne, 2013.

Mounce, Robert H. *The Book of Revelation.* Grand Rapids: Eerdmans, 1977.

Muir, Steven. "Vivid Imagery in Galatians 3:1—Roman Rhetoric, Street Announcing, Graffiti, and Crucifixions." *Biblical Theology Bulletin* 44 (2014): 76–86.

Murphy-O'Connor, Jerome. *Paul: His Story.* Oxford: Oxford University Press, 2006.

Myers, Jacob M. *I and II Esdras.* Garden City, NY: Doubleday, 1974.

Niang, Aliou Cissé. "Seeing and Hearing Jesus Christ Crucified in Galatians 3:1 under Watchful Imperial Eyes." In *Text, Image, and Christians in the*

Graeco-Roman World, ed. Aliou Cissé Niang and Carolyn Osiek, 160–82. Eugene, OR: Pickwick, 2012.

Niccolini, Fausto. *Le Case ed il Monumenti di Pompei; Volume 3, Part 1.* Naples: 1890.

Nongbri, Brent. "The Limits of Palaeographic Dating of Literary Papyri: Some Observations on the Date and Provenance of P. Bodmer II (P66)." *Museum Helveticum* 71 (2014): 1–35.

Osiek, Carolyn, and David L. Balch. *Families in the New Testament World: Households and House Churches.* Louisville: Westminster John Knox, 1997.

Pearson, Birger A. *Gnosticism and Christianity in Roman and Coptic Egypt.* New York: T & T Clark, 2004.

Pirson, Felix. "Rented Accommodation at Pompeii: The Insula Arriana Polliana." In *Domestic Space in the Roman World: Pompeii and Beyond*, ed. R. Lawrence and A. Wallace-Hadrill, 165–81. Supplement Series 22. Portsmouth, RI: Journal of Roman Archaeology, 1997.

Price, Jonathan J. "Ossuary of Iesous Aloth with Greek Inscription, 1 c. CE." In *Corpus Inscriptionum Iudaeae/Palaestinae, Volume 1.2: Jerusalem, Part 2: 705–1120*, ed. Hannah M. Cotton, Leah di Segni, Werner Eck, Benjamine Isaac, Alla Kushnir-Stein, Haggai Misgav, Jonathan J. Price, and Ada Yardeni, 501–2. Berlin: de Gruyter, 2012.

———. "Ossuary with Greek Letters and Byzantine crux immissa, 1 c. CE." In *Corpus Inscriptionum Iudaeae/Palaestinae, Volume 1.2: Jerusalem, Part 2: 705–1120*, ed. Hannah M. Cotton, Leah di Segni, Werner Eck, Benjamine Isaac, Alla Kushnir-Stein, Haggai Misgav, Jonathan J. Price, and Ada Yardeni, 289. Berlin: de Gruyter, 2012.

Price, Jonathan J. and Hannah M. Cotton. "Ossuary of Yehuda with Hebrew/Aramaic Inscription, 1 c. CE." In *Corpus Inscriptionum Iudaeae/ Palaestinae, Volume 1.2: Jerusalem, Part 2: 705–1120*, ed. Hannah M. Cotton, Leah di Segni, Werner Eck, Benjamine Isaac, Alla Kushnir-Stein, Haggai Misgav, Jonathan J. Price, and Ada Yardeni, 274–75. Berlin: de Gruyter, 2012.

Price, Simon. "Religious Mobility in the Roman Empire." *Journal of Roman Studies* 96 (2006): 1–19.

Ramsay, William M. *The Letters to the Seven Churches of Asia and Their Place in the Plan of the Apocalypse.* London: Hodder & Stoughton, 1904.

———. *St Paul the Traveller and the Roman Citizen.* London: Hodder & Stoughton, 1895.

Ramsey, Boniface. "A Note on the Disappearance of the Good Shepherd from Early Christian Art." *Harvard Theological Review* 76 (1983): 375–78.

Rollston, Christopher. "Review of *The Jesus Discovery: The New Archaeological Find That Reveals the Birth of Christianity*, by James D. Tabor and Simcha Jacobovici (New York: Simon and Schuster, 2012)." *Rollston Epigraphy: Ancient Inscriptions from the Levantine World.* April 12, 2012. http://www.rollstonepigraphy.com/?p=497.

Samuelsson, Gunnar. *Crucifixion in Antiquity: An Inquiry into the Background and Significance of the New Testament Terminology of Crucifixion.* Tübingen: Mohr Siebeck, 2013.

Sanders, Jack T. *Schismatics, Sectarians, Dissidents, Deviants: The First One Hundred Years of Jewish-Christian Relations.* London: SCM Press, 1993.

Schmidt, Carl. *The Books of Jeu and the Untitled Text in the Bruce Codex.* Translated by Violet MacDermot. Leiden: Brill, 1978.

Schmidt, Daryl. "The Jesus Tradition in the Common Life of the Early Church." In *Common Life in the Early Church: Essays Honoring Graydon E Snyder*, ed. Julian V. Hills et al., 135–46. Harrisburg, PA: Trinity Press International, 1998.

Shanks, Hershel. "New Analysis of the Crucified Man." *Biblical Archaeology Review* (November–December 1985): 20–21.

Shaw, David M. "Called to Bless: Considering an Under-appreciated Aspect of 'Doing Good' in 1 Peter." Paper presented to the Social World of the New Testament Seminar of the British New Testament Conference, Manchester, UK, 2014.

Sheckler, Everingham, and Winn Leith. "The Crucifixion Conundrum and the Santa Sabina Doors." *Harvard Theological Review* 103 (2010): 67–88.

Small, Alastair M. "Urban, Suburban and Rural Religion in the Roman Period." In *The World of Pompeii*, ed. John J. Dobbins and Pedar W. Foss, 184–211. New York: Routledge, 2007.

Snyder, Graydon F. *Ante pacem: Archaeological Evidence of Church Life before Constantine.* Rev. ed. Macon, GA: Mercer University Press, 2003.

Speaight, Robert. "Review of F. van der Meer, *Early Christian Art* (London: Faber, 1969)." *Journal of the Royal Society of Arts* 117 (1969): 295.

Spier, Jeffrey. *Ancient Gems and Finger Rings: Catalogue of the Collections.* Malibu, CA: The J. Paul Getty Museum, 1992.

———. "The Earliest Christian Art." In *Picturing the Bible: The Earliest Christian Art*, ed. Jeffrey Spier, 1–24. New Haven, CT: Yale University Press, 2007.

———. *Late Antique and Early Christian Gems.* Wiesenbaden: Reichert, 2007.

———. "Late Antique and Early Christian Gems: Some Unpublished Examples." In *"Gems of Heaven": Recent Research on Engraved Gemstones in Late Antiquity c. AD 200–600*, ed. Chris Entwistle and Noël Adams, 193–207. London: British Museum Press, 2011.

Stark, Rodney. *For the Glory of God: How Monotheism Led to Reformations, Science, Witch-Hunts, and the End of Slavery.* Princeton, NJ: Princeton University Press, 2003.

Sukenik, E. L. "The Earliest Records of Christianity." *American Journal of Archaeology* 51 (1947): 351–65.

Sweet, John P. M. *Revelation.* Philadelphia: Westminster, 1979.

Tabbernee, William. "Asia Minor and Cyprus." In *Early Christianity in Contexts: An Exploration across Cultures and Continents*, ed. William Tabbernee, 261–320. Grand Rapids: Baker Academic, 2014.

———. "Christian Inscriptions from Phrygia." In *New Documents Illustrating Early Christianity*, ed. G. H. R. Horsley and S. R. Llewellyn, 3:128–39. Grand Rapids: Eerdmans, 1978.

———, ed. *Early Christianity in Contexts: An Exploration across Cultures and Continents*. Grand Rapids: Baker Academic, 2014.

———. "Early Montanism and Voluntary Martyrdom." *Colloquium* 17 (1985): 33–44.

———. *Fake Prophecy and Polluted Sacraments*. Leiden: Brill, 2007.

———. *Montanist Inscriptions and Testimonia: Epigraphic Sources Illustrating the History of Montanism*. Macon, GA: Mercer University Press, 1997.

Tabor, James D., and Simcha Jacobovici. *The Jesus Discovery: The Resurrection Tomb That Reveals the Birth of Christianity*. New York: Simon and Schuster, 2012.

Tajfel, Henri, and John Turner. "An Integrative Theory of Intergroup Conflict." In *Intergroup Relations: Essential Readings*, ed. Michael A. Hogg and Dominic Abrams, 94–109. Philadelphia: Psychology Press, 2001.

Taylor, John H. *Death and the Afterlife in Ancient Egypt*. London: The Trustees of the British Museum (The British Museum Press), 2001.

Thompson, Michael. "The Holy Internet: Communication between Churches in the First Christian Generation." In *The Gospels for All Christians: Rethinking the Gospel Audiences*, ed. Richard Bauckham, 49–70. Grand Rapids: Eerdmans, 1998.

Thomsen, Peter. *Die lateinischen und griechischen Inschriften der Stadt Jerusalem und ihrer nächsten Umgebung*. Leipzig: J. C. Hinrichs, 1922.

Turner, E. G. *Greek Manuscripts of the Ancient World*. 2nd ed. London: Institute of Classical Studies, 1987.

Tzaferis, Vasilios. "Early Christian Churches at Magen." In *Ancient Churches Revealed*, ed. Yoram Tsafrir, 283–85. Jerusalem: Israel Exploration Society, 1993.

Valeva, Julia. "Les tombeaux ornés de croix et des chrismes peints." In *Acta XIII congressus internationalis archaeologiae christianae Split–Poreč (25. 9.–1. 10. 1994)*, ed. N. Cambi and E. Marin, 761–86. Città del Vaticano: Split, 1998.

Valeva, Julia, and Athanosios K. Vionis. "The Balkan Peninsula." In *Early Christianity in Contexts: An Exploration across Cultures and Continents*, ed. William Tabbernee, 321–78. Grand Rapids: Baker Academic, 2014.

Varone, Antonio. *Presenze guidaiche e cristiane a Pompei.* Naples: M. D'Auria Editore, 1979.

Vermaseren, Maarten Josef. *Corpus inscriptionum et monumentorum religionis Mithriacae.* 2 vols. The Hague: Martinus Nijhoff, 1956–60.

Viladesau, Richard. *The Beauty of the Cross: The Passion of Christ in Theology and the Arts, from the Catacombs to the Eve of the Renaissance.* Oxford: Oxford University Press, 2006.

Volf, Miroslav. "Soft Difference: Theological Reflections on the Relation between Church and Culture in 1 Peter." *Ex Auditu* 10 (1994): 15–30.

Waelkens, Marc. *Die Kleinasiatischen Türsteine: Typologische und epigraphische Untersuchungen der kleinasiatischen Grabreliefs mit Scheintür.* Mainz am Rhein: Verlag Philipp von Zabern, 1986.

Wallace, Daniel B. *Greek Grammar beyond the Basics: An Exegetical Syntax of the New Testament.* Grand Rapids: Zondervan, 1996.

Wallace-Hadrill, Andrew. "*Domus* and *Insulae* in Rome: Families and Housefuls." In *Early Christian Families in Context: An Interdisciplinary Dialogue*, ed. David L. Balch and Carolyn Osiek, 3–18. Grand Rapids: Eerdmans, 2003.

———. *Houses and Society in Pompeii and Herculaneum.* Princeton, NJ: Princeton University Press, 1994.

Wilken, Robert Louis. *The Christians as the Romans Saw Them.* New Haven, CT: Yale University Press, 1984.

Williams, Michael Allen. *Rethinking "Gnosticism": An Argument for Dismantling a Dubious Category.* Princeton, NJ: Princeton University Press, 1996.

Williams, Travis. *Good Works in 1 Peter: Negotiating Social Conflict and Christian Identity in the Greco-Roman World.* Tübingen: Mohr Siebeck, 2014.

————. *Persecution in 1 Peter: Differentiating and Contextualizing Early Christian Suffering.* Leiden: Brill, 2012.

Winter, Bruce W. *After Paul Left Corinth: The Influence of Secular Ethics and Social Change.* Grand Rapids: Eerdmans, 2001.

Wright, N. T. *Paul and the Faithfulness of God.* Minneapolis: Fortress Press, 2013.

Yarbro Collins, Adela. *The Apocalypse.* Wilmington, DE: Michael Glazier, 1983.

Yarbrough, Oliver Larry. "The Shadow of an Ass: On Reading the Alexamenos Graffito." In *Text, Image, and Christians in the Graeco-Roman World*, ed. Aliou Cissé Niang and Carolyn Osiek, 239–54. Eugene, OR: Pickwick, 2012.

Zias, Joseph, and Eliezer Sekeles. "The Crucified Man from Giv'at ha-Mivtar: A Reappraisal." *Israel Exploration Journal* 35 (1985): 22–27.

Index of Subjects

Index of Modern Authors

Index of Ancient Sources

Index of Locations

Alexandria, 30, 62, 62n2, 164

Ancyra, 117n80

Antioch, 159

Asia Minor, 26, 88, 90, 92, 92n30, 155, 164–65, 168–69

Caesarea, 155

Carsamba Valley, 25

Carthage (Northern Africa), 151, 164

Corinth, 24, 133, 144–45, 145n30, 147

Cyprus, 27n14; Yoronisos Island (off the coast of Cyprus), 121n2

Eastern Mediterranean, 103n49

Egypt, 15–16, 140, 154, 157, 174

Ephesus, 144–45, 145n30, 159

Gaza, 101, 164

Greece, 47n49

Herculaneum, 32, 45, 115–17, 123, 130–31, 134–36, 138, 144; House of the Bicentenary, 32, 130–31, 134–35

Iberian Peninsula, 92, 164, 182

Israel, 14

Italy, 46

Jerusalem, 3, 22–23, 49–55, 52n5, 58, 58n16, 67–69, 82, 102, 146n34, 154, 164

Judea, 32n24, 146n34, 147n35

Mediterranean basin, 165–66, 174, 179, 186

Mount Vesuvius, 9, 121, 123, 138, 142–43, 146n34, 174